Contents

Introduction

A good working relationship between architect and client is crucial to the success of most projects, and the confidence generated by the existence at the outset of an agreement that clearly and formally identifies services, costs and procedures will underpin that relationship and minimise the potential for misunderstanding and dispute. The RIBA *Code of Professional Conduct* requires architects, when entering into an agreement for professional services, to:

> 'have defined beyond reasonable doubt and recorded the terms of the engagement including the scope of the service, the allocation of responsibilities and any limitation of liability, the method of calculation of remuneration and the provision for termination.'

On 1 July 1992 the RIBA published the new *Standard Form of Agreement for the Appointment of an Architect* (SFA/(92) as a replacement for *Architect's Appointment* ('The Blue Book'). The documents were formulated by a working group comprising the RIBA, RIAS, RSUA and ACA. In 1993 a separate suite of SFA documents was published for Design and Build projects in two versions (*Employer Client* and *Contractor Client*) together with a Guide (*SFA Design and Build Guide*). SFA/92 is published in an RIBA edition and a RIAS edition, suitable for commissions carried out under Scots law.

The aim of this Guide is to provide architects with advice on the use and completion of the SFA documents, but clients who are considering the appointment of an architect and wish to inform themselves about architects' services and conditions of appointment will also find the Guide helpful and relevant. Guidance for clients on architects' fees is published in *Engaging an Architect: Guidance for Clients on Fees* (1994, an RIBA 'yellow book').

The SFA/92 documents

SFA/92 consists of a Memorandum of Agreement, Conditions, and four schedules. These are for recording:
- information to be supplied by the client;
- the services to be provided by the architect;
- the way payment for the services is to be calculated, charged and made;
- details of the appointment (if any) of other consultants and specialists.

An alternative schedule of services for commissions connected with Historic Building work is published separately, as is a schedule of supplementary services for Community Architecture projects. Each document is described in this Guide, together with notes on its use and completion, and a full set of worked examples is included as Appendix 1.

The CDM Regulations 1994

The SFA documents were formulated before the introduction of the CDM Regulations, which became effective on 31 March 1995. In response, the RIBA published a special 'CDM Supplement' to be used in conjunction with SFA/92. The Supplement, which contains additional Definitions, Conditions and Services relevant to the Regulations, is incorporated by making appropriate additions to the Memorandum of Agreement. It is then attached to the other SFA documents which comprise the Agreement. A specimen CDM Supplement is included as Appendix 3 of this Guide.

The RIBA also publishes a guide for clients which describes their statutory obligations under the CDM Regulations and discusses the implications in a constructive way. The guide (another 'yellow book') is entitled *Engaging an Architect: Guidance for Clients on Health and Safety – the CDM Regulations 1994*. An indicative fee scale for Planning Supervisor services is included.

Memorandum of Agreement

Use

The Memorandum of Agreement cannot be completed and signed until the services and costs have been agreed and the details set out in the Schedules. The Conditions and Schedules must be attached to the Memorandum and clearly identified on each page as belonging to it. They are then incorporated into the Agreement by reference.

The Memorandum identifies the Parties, states their intentions and agreement concerning the nature, scope and cost of the professional services to be provided. The Recitals identify the project and its location and refer to the Conditions and Schedules. The Memorandum will usually be signed as a simple contract, but some Clients may require it to be executed as a Deed. An alternative version of the Memorandum is included for this purpose.

Completion

The names and addresses of the parties should be inserted. A brief description of the project should be given and the site identified.

Liability

Points of agreement 5 and 6 provide an opportunity to limit the liability of the Architect to the Client in period of time, in maximum amount of damages payable, and to a fair contribution depending on responsibility. The Limitation Act 1980 refers to periods of 6 years and 12 years from the date of a breach of contract, simple or deed respectively. In Scotland, the Prescription and Limitation Act 1973 refers to a period of 5 years from the date of discovery of damage. Where Architects provide a service which includes for work stages J–L as described in Part Three of the Conditions, practical completion under the building contract may not be achieved until a number of years after the date of the SFA, and this should be borne in mind in discussions about a suitable limitation period. Damages for breach of contract are unlimited in law and may include consequential losses. In no circumstances should a figure be entered under 6.2 which exceeds the insurance cover taken out.

Signing the Agreement as a simple contract

The Agreement should be signed by both parties and the date of the Agreement entered when this has been done.

Execution as a Deed

If the Client insists on the Agreement being executed as a Deed, the alternative version of the Memorandum should be used. A Deed no longer needs formally to be sealed. The only requirement is that the document is executed and delivered as a Deed and expressed to be so. However, some Clients, as a matter of tradition or for other non-legal reasons, still like to affix their seal under their names (or the names of their officers).

Signatures to the Deed

In the case of incorporated bodies (limited companies etc), *either* two directors *or* one director and the company secretary should sign the Deed. Their signatures need not be witnessed. (Note, however, that this method is not valid for local authorities or certain other bodies incorporated by Act of Parliament or by charter if exempted under S.718(2) of the Companies Act 1985.) In the case of a partnership, all the partners must sign unless one of them is authorised *by Deed* to represent them all.

Under the law of England and Wales, the signatures of private individuals, sole practitioners, or partners in a firm must be witnessed. A separate version of the alternative form for use in Scotland is included in the RIAS edition of SFA/92, because under Scots law there are differing requirements for attestation, and some other variations.

Architects should bear in mind that the main effect of execution as a Deed under English law is to extend their liability under contract from 6 to 12 years. Under Scots law, execution of a probative document extends the liability period from 5 years to 20 years.

Notes for Architects

Check the details of appointment

Before signature, check the SFA documents carefully to make sure that they fully and accurately record the services to be provided and the basis for payment. Scrutinise any amendments and make sure they have been initialled and dated by both parties.

Check the documents issued

Before sending or presenting the documents to the Client for signature, refer to the checklist of documents printed on the inside front cover of the SFA pack, and tick the documents being used for this appointment.

Number of copies

Agree with the Client how many certified copies of the SFA are to be made, who is to receive them, and who is to retain the original.

The Conditions of Appointment

Use

The Conditions have been conceived as an entity, and the wording should be regarded as standard. They are in four parts. Part One applies to all commissions, but Parts Two and Three only apply where the service entails design and/or administration of the building contract and site inspection. Part Four only applies where consultants and specialists are to be appointed.

Defined words and phrases are given initial capital letters wherever they appear in the SFA documents. Additional Definitions and Conditions relevant to the CDM Regulations are given in the SFA CDM Supplement (Appendix 3).

Part One: **Conditions Common to all Commissions**

Governing law

In Condition 1.1.1, delete the options that are not to apply. Note that this will have implications for Condition 1.8 (Dispute resolution).

Architect's obligations

Note that the Architect's authority (Cond. 1.2.3) is related to approval obtained from the Client at points or dates referred to in the Timetable supplied by the Client.

Material alteration of the Services requires the consent of the Client (Cond. 1.2.4), and the Architect is obliged to inform the Client of any incompatibility between Requirements, Budget and Timetable (Cond. 1.2.5). Although the Architect does not warrant completion to the Timetable (Cond. 1.3.7), this document is obviously significant from the outset.

Client's obligations

Note that the Client is obliged to provide information specified in Schedule One, further reasonably necessary information, and decisions and approvals to enable the Architect to comply with the Timetable (Conds. 1.3.2 to 1.3.6). Although the Client accepts that the

Architect will rely on information supplied (Cond. 1.3.4), the Architect must nevertheless exercise reasonable skill and care.

Payment

Note that the basis and timing of payments, whether fees, expenses or disbursements, relates to the entries in Schedule Three. This schedule should be completed with great care.

Condition 1.5.4 refers to time rates, and mileage rates for cars, being revised at 12-monthly intervals from the date of the appointment unless stated otherwise in Schedule Three. (Conflicts with office policy and fiscal years might make revision necessary.)

Condition 1.5.6 applies where fees are on a lump sum basis, and allows for a revision of this sum in accordance with Schedule Three. If applicable, a provision should be included in Schedule Three. Condition 1.6.3 allows the Architect to suspend services where the Client has failed to pay fees in accordance with the agreed schedule of payments set out in Schedule Three.

Dispute resolution

Condition 1.8.4 accepts that disputes may, with the agreement of the parties, be resolved by negotiation, conciliation or litigation. Otherwise, there will be recourse to arbitration, which, under Condition 1.8.3 in Scotland or Northern Ireland, will not commence for 28 days to allow for settlement by negotiation. Additionally, in Scotland and Northern Ireland the parties may elect to refer disputes to the respective professional bodies for an opinion (Cond. 1.8.2).

Conditions 1.8.1 and 1.8.1S are alternative arbitration clauses applying to England and Wales, Northern Ireland or Scotland respectively. Which is to apply depends on the appropriate deletion under Condition 1.1.1 (Governing law).

Part Two:	Conditions Specific to the Design of Building Projects

Architect's obligations

Note that Condition 2.1.2. states that the Architect shall advise on appropriate procurement methods. This is an obligation regardless of whether the Client takes advice from elsewhere.

Client's obligations

The Client must give instructions for the making of applications for permissions and approvals, both statutory and non-statutory, and pay fees and charges arising (Cond. 2.2.1).

Condition 2.2.2 obliges the Client to inform the Architect before the Agreement is signed whether any third parties have or are likely to acquire an interest in the project.

Condition 2.2.3 imposes an obligation on the Client not to require the Architect to enter into collateral agreements with third parties which impose obligations more onerous than those under the *Standard Form of Agreement for the Appointment of an Architect.*

Condition 2.2.4 requires the Client to confirm the procurement method which is to be adopted. Obviously some assumptions will need to be made at the time the Agreement is executed, and some subsequent renegotiation may be necessary.

Copyright

Condition 2.3.1 gives the client the right to carry out the project subject to certain provisos, one of which is payment to the Architect of any fees and expenses due. Under Condition

1.7.1 the Architect retains the copyright both in respect of documents and the completed work.

Conditions 2.3.2 and 2.3.3 deal with schemes commissioned under partial services, and where consent by the Architect, or payment of additional fees, may be necessary.

Condition 2.3.4 is a safeguard for Architects in cases where design information is applied beyond the intended purposes.

Part Three: **Conditions Specific to the Administration of the Building Contract and Inspection of the Works**

Architect's obligations
Condition 3.1.1 requires the Architect to confirm in writing at the date of the Appointment the pattern of visits to the Works expected to be necessary. This should include a contingency for site visits additional to those which are foreseeable as routine or predictive inspections. If it becomes necessary to vary the expected pattern of visits, the Client must be informed of this in writing and also of any variation in fees resulting (Conds. 3.1.2 and 3.1.3).

Condition 3.1.4 authorises the Architect to make alterations to the approved design during construction without the consent of the Client only in an emergency and subject to immediate confirmation in writing. Otherwise the Client's consent must be obtained prior to any material design alteration.

Client's obligations
The Client is required to employ a contractor under a separate contract and to undertake to hold him directly responsible for all matters concerned with carrying out the Works (Conds. 3.2.1 to 3.2.3). The contractor is also held directly responsible for all matters of site safety which are his legal concern (Cond. 3.2.2).

The Client is required to undertake that the contractor will be similarly bound where the Architect is required to enter into a collateral agreement (Cond. 3.2.4).

Site staff
Under Condition 3.3.1 the Architect is required to recommend the appointment of site staff, where necessary, and confirm in writing the expected duration of their employment, who is to appoint and pay them, and how their costs are to be recovered (Cond. 3.3.2). Site staff are to be under the direction and control of the Architect (Cond. 3.3.3).

Part Four: **Conditions Specific to the Appointment of Consultants and Specialists (where the Architect is Lead Consultant)**

Consultants
The Architect, as Lead Consultant, must identify professional services which require the appointment of other consultants (Cond. 4.1.1). Their nomination may be by either party, subject to mutual acceptance. Their appointment and payment will be a direct matter for the Client (Cond. 4.1.2). Nomination may be at any time, but Schedule Four is the formal recognition of the need for appointment. The Architect is to confirm in writing the services required from the consultants (Cond. 4.1.3).

Where the Architect is required to enter into a collateral agreement (Cond. 4.1.4), the Client is required to undertake that all consultants will be similarly bound.

Condition 4.1.6 obliges the Client to incorporate the Architect's authority as lead consultant into the conditions of appointment for all other consultants and provide the Architect with a copy of their respective conditions (Conds. 4.1.5, 4.1.6).

The Client is required to undertake to hold consultants directly responsible for their own work (Cond. 4.1.7), but this does not affect the authority of the Architect as administrator of the building contract (Cond. 4.1.8). The Architect remains responsible for obtaining necessary information from consultants, and for coordinating and integrating their work into the overall design (Cond. 4.1.5).

Specialists
Specialist firms with a design responsibility, whether employed direct by the Client or indirectly through the contractor, may be nominated by Architect or Client subject to mutual acceptance (Cond. 4.2.1). The Architect is obliged to confirm in writing to the Client the services to be provided by specialists as known at the time of the Appointment (Cond. 4.2.2).

The Client is required to undertake that all specialists will be similarly bound where the Architect agrees to enter into a collateral agreement (Cond. 4.2.3).

The Client is required to undertake to hold specialists directly responsible for their own work (Cond. 4.2.5), but this does not affect the responsibility of the Architect for the coordination and integration of consultants' work into the overall design.

Notes for Architects

Amendments
It is in the interests of both Client and Architect that the wording of the Conditions is regarded as standard, but if amendments have to be conceded, whether additions or deletions, each should be initialled and dated by both parties. In each case the amendment should be clearly expressed and legible, and its intention clear. Where the Client insists on material alterations, it is advisable to seek legal advice.

Terminology
The Definitions only refer to words and phrases that are used in the SFA. A Client who is unfamiliar with building terminology may need explanations of these and many others in the course of discussions.

Site staff
At this early stage it will not be easy to predict the staff required, but it should be possible to indicate the categories of staff to be appointed and an approximate duration of employment. There is provision in Schedule Four to record details of their employment as known at the date of the Agreement. Subsequent appointments will need to be agreed with the Client and confirmed in writing.

Date and initial the document
For the sake of certainty of incorporation, make sure that the Conditions foldout is initialled and dated at the foot of the first page.

Schedule One

Use

Schedule One concerns information to be supplied by the Client and is in three parts, corresponding to the Parts of the Conditions. Refer to the worked example in Appendix 1.

Part One applies to all commissions, and the standard items which the Client is to supply (Requirements, Budget, and Timetable) are pre-printed. This information is essential for the proper application of the Conditions, and it will be for the parties to agree on the extent and detail of what is needed. Anything else needed is to be described under *Other matters*.

Part Two relates to services for the design of building projects, under *Plan of Work* stages A–H. Again, the items on which information is most commonly required are pre-printed and anything else needed is added under *Other matters*.

Part Three relates to services connnected with contract administration and inspection of the Works. This Part is needed only when appointment includes these services. It should be specified in the space provided which items of information relating to contract administration and site inspection are to be supplied by the Client. Although Architects are entitled to rely on the accuracy and adequacy of information provided by the Client (Cond. 1.3.4), they will still be vulnerable to allegations of negligence for overlooking something that a competent Architect should have noticed.

Completion

In Part One, the need for the Client to supply Requirements, Budget and Timetable should be acknowledged (tick these items), and precise reference inserted to other documents which will carry the detailed information. These fundamental elements should be attainable as well as compatible and this should be checked at the time of appointment, since, once accepted, failure to meet them could put an Architect in breach of contract.

The *Other matters* section should be completed as appropriate.

Part Two is for recording the information concerning the site and any buildings that is to be provided by the Client or his advisers. The Client has an obligation to provide information, but is unlikely to know what is *necessary* unless it is specifically requested. Architects should be sure to tell the Client what is required.

The *Other matters* section should be completed as appropriate.

Part Three is for specifying any other relevant information specific to contract administration and site inspection to be supplied by the Client.

Any of the pre-printed items in Parts One and Two which it has been agreed to exclude should be deleted.

Notes for Architects

> **Prompt supply of information**
> The supply of information by the Client is critical to the success of the project. Explain the importance of its being supplied promptly and fully. It is in no one's interests, and a waste of time, for Architects to become involved in making investigations concerning matters that are outside their normal competence.
>
> **Date and initial the document**
> For the sake of certainty of incorporation, make sure that the Schedule is initialled and dated at the foot of the page.

Schedule Two

Use

Schedule Two is used to identify the services to be provided by the Architect. A wide range of services is itemised under the headings:
(1) Design Skills;
(2) Consultancy Services;
(3) Buildings/Sites;
(4) All Commissions.

The items listed under (4) will be common to all services whether specifically project-related or not. The Services Specific to Building Projects are set out under *Plan of Work* stages A–B to K–L, and the coloured areas indicate items which, unless deleted, will be included as standard for the agreed fee.

Completion

Schedule Two (sheet 6a)
Services in the columns 1–3 will be selected by first ringing round the heading number appropriate, and then ringing round the reference number for particular selected items. Column 4 will always be applicable, and the first two items are printed ringed round.

Schedule Two (sheets 6b and 6c)
Services in the columns will be selected by first ringing round the relevant Work Stages. All items within the coloured area below the selected headings are automatically included. Items within the coloured area not to be included should be struck out. Items not within a coloured area which are to be included should be ringed round.

Quantity surveyor
If a QS is not appointed, C.03, D.03, E.03, F–G.03 and .06, and K–L.03 should be struck through to leave the alternative (with an A affix) whereby the Architect will provide/update the cost estimate, eg C.03A, D.03A etc.

Bills of quantities
The basic services assume that bills of quantities will be prepared by a QS. If this is not the case, F–G.03 should be struck through. If the Architect is to prepare schedules of rates, works or quantities etc for tendering purposes, the alternative F–G.03A will apply.

Valuations
The basic services assume that a QS will prepare valuations for certification by the Architect. If this is *not* the case, and the Architect is to do this within the basic fee, K–L.15 should be ringed round.

Other consultants
The basic services assume that other consultants are appointed and that the Architect will incorporate their work into the overall design. If consultants are *not* appointed, C.02, D.02, E.02, F–G.04 and H.03 should be struck through. In the absence of other consultants, the Architect will undertake the services which have an A affix.

Planning applications
The basic services assume that the Architect prepares an application for full planning permission only (D.11) and that the Client submits it. If the Architect is to submit as well as prepare an application, D.15 should be ringed round. Where multiple planning applications are to be prepared and submitted, D.16 and D.17 should be ringed round. If the Architect is to revise and resubmit planning applications, D.19 and D.20 should be ringed round.

Statutory approvals

The basic services assume that the Architect prepares applications for approvals under Building Acts/Regulations etc and that the Client submits them. If the Architect is to apply for the approvals, E.07 should be ringed round.

Note that E.04A and .07A, which concern building notice procedures, do not apply in Scotland and will require deletion as appropriate.

Tendering

The basic services assume that single stage selective tendering will be adopted. In certain other circumstances it may be advisable to move out of the coloured area, and make consequential deletions as appropriate.

Should tenders come in above the budget, and the Architect is to be involved in negotiations over price, H.05 and H.06 or H.07, outside the coloured area, should be ringed round as commissioned. These services entail additional fees.

Client approvals

Note that the basic services listed for stages C, D and E all have included as their last item (C.04, D.12 and E.06) the requirement to obtain the Client's approval before proceeding to the next work stage (under Conditions 1.2.3 and 2.1.1). An architect who fails to do this might be held to be working in excess of his or her agreed authority and the work regarded as undertaken at the architect's risk.

Notes for Architects

> **Checking**
>
> It is essential to complete this Schedule carefully so that all inclusions and exclusions are correctly and clearly indicated.
>
> **Planning applications**
>
> As part of the basic services under Stages D and E, the Architect only *prepares* applications for planning permission and Building Regulations approvals. This is because submitting the application requires an accompanying cheque from the Client, often a matter beyond the Architect's control.
>
> **Date and initial the document**
>
> For the sake of certainty of incorporation, make sure that the Schedule Two foldout is initialled and dated at the foot of the first page.

Alternative/supplementary schedules

Alternative/supplementary schedules of services for use with commissions relating to Historic Buildings, and Community Architecture are published separately. Specimen documents are included (Appendix 2). Additional services relevant to the CDM Regulations are given in the SFA CDM Supplement (Appendix 3).

Schedule Three

Use

Schedule Three is for setting out the way payment for the agreed services is calculated, charged and paid. Refer to the worked example of this Schedule in Appendix 1.

Completion

(1) Fees
The fee basis for the services to be provided should be set out. This might be simply:
- Basic services plus services _____ at 5% of Total Construction Cost
- Services for a lump sum of £ _____
- All other services to be time-charged

(2) Time charges
Any formula to be used to calculate time charges should be set out. If time rates are to apply, it should be specified whether these are hourly, daily or on some other basis, and whether per individual or per category of staff.

It is prudent to include provision for revising time rates during the course of a project. In the space provided, there should be inserted:
- the date at which salaries are normally reviewed, *or*
- the anniversary date of the appointment.

(3) Expenses
List the expenses to be charged and fill in details of cost and/or percentage.

(4) Disbursements
Where the Architect makes disbursements on the Client's behalf, insert a charge for administration, or use some agreed formula.

(5) Payment in instalments
Agree with the Client a programme for payment, and set this out in the space provided. It might be:
- periodic, eg with time-charged work invoiced monthly; *or*
- in tranches, eg a lump sum payable in four equal instalments due on specified dates; *or*
- related to completion of work stages.

See the example programmes for payment set out in Section 4 of this Guide.

(6) Site staff
Where Architects use their own employees as site staff, a time-charged fee might be appropriate, in line with (2) above. If staff have to be engaged specially for the project, it might be possible to recover the cost of their annual salary plus a charge for administration.

Site staff expenses should be confirmed in (3) above with details of any special payments, eg for accommodation or living allowances. A revision date should be added.

(7) Interest on overdue accounts
Base rates tend to fluctuate, so it is sensible for a recognised rate (a lending bank's, for example) to be specified, plus a mark-up.

VAT, where applicable, is charged on all fees and expenses.

Notes for Architects

Fee apportionment
The arrangements to apply must be spelt out in Schedule Three. See also the example programmes for payment in Section 4 of this Guide.

Date and initial the document
For the sake of certainty of incorporation, make sure that the Schedule is initialled and dated at the foot of the page.

Schedule Four

Use

Schedule Four is used to record the details of appointment of other consultants and specialists where the Architect is lead consultant and, as far as is possible, of any site staff envisaged.

Under Part Four of the Conditions the Architect is required to identify, and confirm in writing to the Client, the professional services for which consultants need to be appointed (Cond. 4.1.1). Consultants may be nominated by Client or Architect, subject to mutual acceptance, but the Client appoints and pays them direct (Cond. 4.1.2).

Completion

Under the appropriate headings, list the services to be provided, and give names and addresses where this is possible.

Although the names of some of the appointees are likely to be unknown at the time the SFA is signed, it should be possible to agree a fee with the proviso that the Client makes additional appointments to provide certain services. It is especially necessary to specify any services to be provided by Consultants which the Client might otherwise expect the Architect to provide.

As the project progresses and the details of appointment become known, these can be confirmed with the Client in a letter (see the Confirmation of Amendment example letter, 2.3.1, in Section 2 of this Guide). It should be countersigned by the Client and retained with the other SFA documents.

Notes for Architects

Architect as Lead Consultant
Schedule Four applies only where the Architect is appointed as Lead Consultant under Condition 4.1.5, with authority over all other appointed consultants and responsibility for coordinating their work and integrating it into the overall design.

Responsibilities
The Client holds the consultants responsible for the competence and performance of their work and for general inspection of its execution (Cond. 4.1.7). Specialists are held responsible for the products and materials they supply, and for the competence, proper execution and performance of their work (Cond. 4.2.5).

Date and initial the document
For the sake of certainty of incorporation, make sure that the Schedule is initialled and dated at the foot of the page.

Four example letters from Architect to Client are given in this Section. All the examples provided in this Guide are simply indicative and should never be copied and issued without proper consideration given to their suitability for the project or the particular circumstances.

2.1 Preliminary Appointment

This letter is appropriate when points of agreement reached in early discussions can be confirmed. Any intention to proceed to a full appointment in due course can also be stated. It assumes that some preliminary services are to be undertaken, although this may not always be the case. A letter of preliminary appointment is included with the set of worked examples of the SFA documents at Appendix 1.

It is sound practice to record points of agreement as soon as possible and have these confirmed in writing by the Client or by countersignature, as in the example letter 2.1.1. This safeguards the negotiating position, demonstrates a businesslike approach, and reduces the risk of misunderstanding.

2.2 Confirmation of Agreement to proceed

This is to confirm agreement to proceed to a full appointment. The letter outlines the agreement reached, and is a useful holding mechanism until the full SFA can be properly completed and signed. (See example 2.2.1.)

2.3 Confirmation of Amendment

Changes will often take place after the SFA has been signed. For example, further consultants or specialists may need to be appointed, site staff engaged, services added or deleted, specific disbursements agreed.

The original signed agreement should *not* be amended or adjusted. The Architect should write to the Client (example 2.3.1) confirming the variation and referring to the signed and dated SFA, and should include a copy of the letter for countersignature and return. This should be added to the original SFA documents and kept safely.

2.4 Activating an Appointment by Stages

Clients may sometimes not wish to commit themselves at the outset to an appointment covering the whole project, preferring to proceed stage by stage as finance, site or other determinants are cleared. The SFA can be completed in such cases, since the Client has the right to terminate the agreement at any stage, and the SFA is sufficiently flexible to allow for fee adjustment.

If the Client insists on proceeding on a stage by stage basis, the SFA documents could be completed for the whole project and each stage to be undertaken could be activated by an instructing letter. Refer to examples 2.4.1 and 2.4.2.

In all cases, the conditions of the SFA should be incorporated by reference.

Example letter 2.1.1   **Preliminary Appointment**

```
[NAME OF PROJECT]

We are writing about the terms of our appointment for this
project.

You have asked us to undertake some preliminary services so
that the project may proceed, and we confirm these as
follows:

.................................................................
.................................................................

It is understood that if you subsequently instruct us to
undertake other preliminary services, you will confirm this
in writing. All these services will be charged on a time
basis at the following rates:

     Principals                    £ ...... per ......
     Senior architectural staff    £ ...... per ......
     Other architectural staff     £ ...... per ......
     Administrative staff          £ ...... per ......

In addition, the following expenses will be charged:

.................................................................
.................................................................

Invoices will be submitted monthly. VAT has to be charged at
the current standard rate on all our fees and expenses.

For the above services to be provided effectively, you will
also need to appoint:

.................................................................
.................................................................

You should note that other financial commitments at this
stage may include:

.................................................................
.................................................................

We will provide these services on the basis of the
Conditions included at Part ..... of the Standard Form of
Agreement for the Appointment of an Architect (SFA/92), a
copy of which is enclosed [if appropriate at this stage].

We envisage that this preliminary appointment will continue
for approximately ..... months while we conclude the
principal appointment under SFA/92. When the principal
Agreement has been entered into, this appointment will be
subsumed into it, and fees invoiced under this letter will
rank as payments on account.

Please confirm your acceptance of the appointment set out in
this letter by signing the enclosed copy and returning it to
us.
```

Example letter 2.2.1   **Confirmation of Agreement to proceed to full Appointment**

```
[NAME OF PROJECT]

We are writing to confirm that we will provide the services
agreed at our recent discussions and as set out in this
letter.

It is agreed that we [name] will provide you [name and
address] with services in connection with [identify project
and location]. In addition, it is agreed that:

(1) Information

You will provide the following information:

............................................................
............................................................

(2) Services

We will provide the following services:
[Describe them briefly.]

............................................................
............................................................

(3) Fees

For these services we will charge a fee of
[Specify and describe basis.]

.............................    ........................
.............................    ........................

plus expenses
[Describe and specify rates etc.]

.............................    ........................
.............................    ........................

We will provide these services in accordance with the
Conditions of the Standard Form of Agreement for the
Appointment of an Architect (SFA), a copy of which is
enclosed [if appropriate at this stage].

(4) Consultants

To assist us in carrying out these services you will appoint
the following consultants:
[List disciplines and names, if agreed at this stage.]

.............................    ........................
.............................    ........................
```

continued

Example letter 2.2.1
continued

(5) Site staff

The following site staff will be required:
[List if names are known, or describe by function.]

....
....

The cost of employing them will be charged to you.

(6) Services by others

The following services are to be provided by others:
[Site surveys, soil investigations etc.]

....
....

You will be charged direct for these services.

(7) Planning submissions

You have accepted that local authority charges for planning and building control submissions fall outside our fees and that you will pay these direct.

(8) Value Added Tax

VAT is chargeable on our fees and expenses at the appropriate rate current at the time of invoicing.

If you agree that this is a correct summary, please sign the enclosed copy of this letter and return it to us. We shall then be in a position to receive your instructions to start work.

We confirm that the intention is to express the above agreement formally in the Standard Form of Agreement for the Appointment of an Architect (SFA/92), and we will be discussing its completion with you or your advisers in the near future.

We are looking forward to working with you on this project.

Example letter 2.3.1   **Confirmation of Amendment**

```
[NAME OF PROJECT]

We refer to the Standard Form of Agreement for the
Appointment of an Architect (SFA/92)

dated ..................
between ......................... [client]
and ........................... [architect]

in respect of the above project.

We confirm that in accordance with Condition ...... of
SFA/92, the following amendment has been agreed:

..........................................................
..........................................................
..........................................................

Please countersign below and return this letter to us. This
recorded amendment will now form part of the Agreement
described above.

Yours faithfully




.........................           .................
(signature of architect)           (date)


.........................           .................
(countersignature by client)       (date)
```

Example letter 2.4.1   **Activating Appointment for certain Stages**

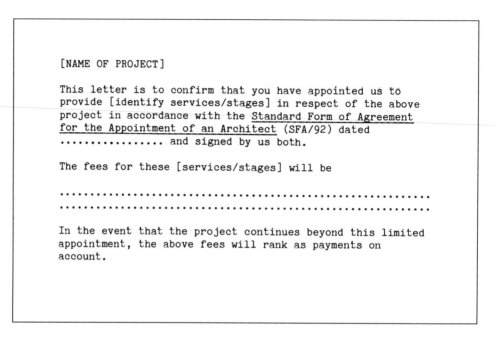

```
[NAME OF PROJECT]

This letter is to confirm that you have appointed us to
provide [identify services/stages] in respect of the above
project in accordance with the Standard Form of Agreement
for the Appointment of an Architect (SFA/92) dated
................ and signed by us both.

The fees for these [services/stages] will be

.............................................................
.............................................................

In the event that the project continues beyond this limited
appointment, the above fees will rank as payments on
account.
```

Example letter 2.4.2   **Activating Appointment for further Stages**

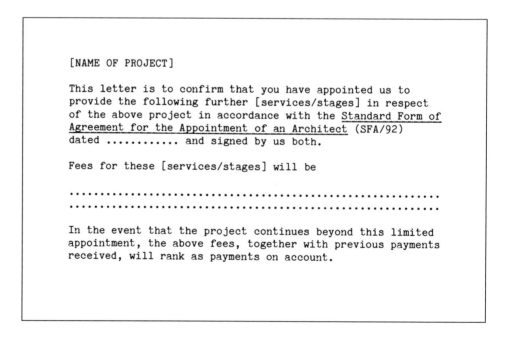

```
[NAME OF PROJECT]

This letter is to confirm that you have appointed us to
provide the following further [services/stages] in respect
of the above project in accordance with the Standard Form of
Agreement for the Appointment of an Architect (SFA/92)
dated ........... and signed by us both.

Fees for these [services/stages] will be

.............................................................
.............................................................

In the event that the project continues beyond this limited
appointment, the above fees, together with previous payments
received, will rank as payments on account.
```

The methods described below may be used in various combinations. Expenses may be included within them or charged separately. Other methods may be proposed by Architect or Client and in each case should be evaluated along the lines of the analyses below.

Before offering or applying any fee method, Architects should carry out a realistic evaluation of the costs to the practice of carrying out the work.

3.1 Percentage Fees

(a) Description

Fees expressed as a percentage of the total construction cost are a useful reference point irrespective of the procurement method finally chosen. Before fees can be calculated, both Client and Architect must establish the services to be provided, the approximate construction budget and the nature of the work, eg whether it is new work or alterations.

(b) When best used

For straightforward building projects where the basic services are to be used.

(c) Available data

The RIBA publishes guidance on fees for architectural services in *Engaging an Architect: Guidance for Clients on Fees* (1994). This 'yellow book' includes fees scales, but it should be pointed out to clients that these are simply indicative.

(d) How applied

Conventionally, on the latest approved revision of the budget until the contract is let; then on the contract sum until the total construction cost is established. Note that there can be difficulties over allocation of office resources where the actual tender figure is considerably lower than the budget or estimate.

(e) Disadvantages/problems

This can be a rough and ready method. It is open to the suggestion that Architects may push up the budget cost to improve their fees. It is also vulnerable to market forces and their influence on contractors' tenders. For dealing with contractors' claims it is sensible to charge separately on a time basis.

3.2 Time charges

(a) Description

All time expended on the project by principals and technical staff is charged at previously agreed rates, revised at stated intervals.

(b) When best used

Any project where the scope of the work cannot be reasonably foreseen or where services cannot be related to the amount of construction. Additional or varied services on an otherwise basic service, open-ended exploration work, feasibility studies, protracted planning negotiations, party wall services etc. are examples where time charges are appropriate.

(c) Available data

None. Rates for principals should reflect the prestige and value of the practice or of the individual.

(d) How applied

A method of calculating time rates for staff is given in the *Architect's Handbook of Practice Management* (1991 edition) in section C3. Rates may be used for bands of staff, eg:

principals

associates

senior professional staff

junior professional staff

technicians

or may be applied for each individual. Whichever method is used should be stated in Schedule Three with a date and method of revision to reflect subsequent changes in salaries and costs. The time of secretarial and administrative staff is not usually charged, but there are times when it should be – for example, when staff are directly engaged to do semi-technical work on a specific project.

(e) Disadvantages/problems

From the Client's point of view, this method of charging may seem open-ended, with the Architect apparently having no incentive to work efficiently. It is advisable to keep the Client informed on the progress of time-charged work, and to agree a figure which is not to be exceeded without prior permission.

3.3 Lump Sum Fees

(a) Description

A total sum of money is agreed for a defined package of services.

(b) When best used

Lump sums are common where the scope of the work can be clearly defined from the outset. It is necessary to define the parameters of services, ie time, project size and cost, where applicable, so that if these are varied by more than a stated amount the lump sum itself may be varied. It is unwise to agree a lump sum with no provision for variation except in the case of a highly focused service to be undertaken over a very short period.

(c) Available data

Not applicable.

(d) How applied

At agreed payment intervals and at agreed proportions. Time charges are often converted to lump sums when the project becomes sufficiently defined. Percentage fees may be similarly converted to lump sums when a firm budget or contract sum is known. In such cases the Client is exchanging a possibly lower fee for certainty of the final outcome.

(e) Disadvantages/problems

A lump sum is a gamble. If it goes wrong, the practice may be severely strained yet have no justification for a revision. Note that this also applies to percentage fees.

3.4 Unit Price Fees

(a) Description

Fees may be agreed on a unit price, for example on the number of hospital beds, number of hotel rooms, on the area of building provided ($£/m^2$), or per building (house, factory, etc).

(b) When best used

When the project is plainly repetitive.

(c) Available data

None.

(d) How applied

Effectively as a form of lump sum.

(e) Disadvantages/problems

See Lump Sum Fees (at 3.3 above).

3.5 Betterment Fees

(a) Description

Fees may be charged as a percentage of the increased value of the Client's property based upon an independent valuation – eg the increased value of the land after the grant of planning permission.

(b) When best used

Where a limited service is required and the value of the Architect's input to the Client would not be recognised by, for example, time-charged fees.

(c) Available data

None.

(d) How applied

Variably.

(e) Disadvantages/problems

This is a speculative approach. A betterment fee aims to secure a proper reward for professional expertise, the full value of which might only become apparent as the project develops. For example, whether or not the scheme proceeds might depend on the architect's skill in handling awkward planning negotiations, or making a successful application for loan sanction, or working with a contractor in preparing a development. No success, no reward.

3.6 Equity Shares

(a) Description

Subject to legal restraints, the Architect agrees to accept equity shares in a project in exchange for carrying some of the financial risks.

(b) When best used

Such agreements are likely to be rare.

(c) Available data

None.

(d) How applied

Variably.

(e) Disadvantages/problems

The finances of architectural practices are seldom structured in a way that would make the risks acceptable.

3.7 Incentive Fees

(a) Description

A fee, often additional to another fee, payable if certain criteria, often time-related, are achieved.

(b) When best used

When special efforts, such as additional staff or equipment,or special staff-related payments, are necessary to achieve the result.

(c) Available data

None.

(d) How applied
Often a lump sum payable on the achievement of a defined standard. The specific performance required must be identified in the SFA documents.

(e) Disadvantages/problems
It is difficult to identify and agree a sum which will both cover the projected additional cost and reward the practice for the possible disruption to its normal procedures. This approach is essentially speculative, however experienced the Architect may be.

3.8 Expenses

(a) At cost
The Architect simply charges whatever it costs the practice, whether the provision is in-house or outside. An example is where the cost of a model made by an in-house department   might be considerably less than the commercial equivalent.

(b) At market rates
The Architect charges market rates even if the practice provides some services in-house, eg printing.

(c) Rolled-up
Expenses included in the fee without being separately expressed. Likely expenses should be estimated and included in the fee. Any that might be costly but are outside the Architect's control, for example special presentations or overseas travel, should be specifically excluded from the rolling-up.

(d) Converted to a percentage
The above comments apply. This method reduces the unknown to the Client. Because the relationship between construction cost and level of expenses is tenuous, the Architect must be prepared to budget and control expenses very carefully.

(e) Lump sum
Much preferred by Clients as giving budget certainty, but obviously dangerous for Architects.

(f) Administrative charge
An administrative charge for keeping records, preparing invoices etc. may be added to methods (a) and (b), and included in methods (c), (d) and (e).

(g) Other methods
Other methods should be considered in the light of the comments above.

(h) Usual charges
Items may be added to or deleted from this list, but those usually regarded as recoverable expenses are listed below.

(i) Reproduction or purchase costs of all documents, drawings, maps, models, photographs and other records, including those used in communication between Architect, Client, consultants and contractors, and for enquiries to contractors, sub-contractors and suppliers. This does not affect any contractual obligation on the part of Architects to supply such documents, and contractors will pay for any prints additional to those to which they are entitled under the contract.

(ii) Hotel and travelling expenses including a mileage allowance for cars at rates stated in Schedule Three, and other payments of this kind.

(iii) Expenses in connection with interviewing and appointing site staff.

(iv) Costs relating to postage, telephone, telex, facsimile and other forms of transmission, air freight and courier services.

(v) Rental and hire charges for specialised equipment, including computers, video equipment etc., where required and agreed by the Client.

(vi) Additional charges for time spent travelling where the distance is beyond an agreed limit.

(j) Exceptional charges
For example, any legal costs in negotiating the appointment where the Client has required unusual changes; the cost of any additional professional indemnity insurance; and the costs associated with any litigation and settlement of claims.

3.9 Disbursements

These are charges properly borne by the Client. Sometimes the Client asks the Architect to pay them and recover the cost later. This should be resisted – Architects are not in the business of lending money – but if they are obliged to comply, they should insist on a handling surcharge. It is advisable to explain to the Client the position with regard to charges such as those payable to local authorities for planning applications, so that the Client is prepared to pay for such disbursements.

If Architects do agree to pay disbursements, they should, when determining an appropriate add-on, carefully consider both the cost (of the money, and of the administration involved) and the risk of not recovering the charge. Examples of disbursements are planning applications fees; expenses incurred in advertising for tenders and resident site staff; and any fees and charges for specialist professional advice, including legal advice, which have been incurred by the Architect with the specific authority of the Client.

3.10 Other Costs

If the Client demands, for example, that the Architect should maintain an office on the Client's premises or on site, or that the Architect should acquire computer equipment to match the Client's, then it will normally be appropriate to charge for these.

It is important to consider the implications in the event of suspension or termination. If the Architect has, for example, engaged staff, rented accommodation or leased equipment specifically for the project and the project aborts, there may be considerable costs which cannot be recovered as fees or expenses. Architects need to be adequately protected against this kind of eventuality.

4   Payment of Fees by Programmed Instalments

To maintain a healthy cashflow, a practice must be able to depend on the substantial fees that arise from building commissions being paid on a regular, preferably monthly, basis. This can be encouraged by suggesting that the Client pays according to a plan of programmed instalments. The certainty of this arrangement is welcomed by most Clients, since payments can be budgeted over a period.

Two example programmes are given below where basic services are being provided: one where there is a single appointment and the other where appointment is to be in stages. Services outside the basic services will probably have been negotiated on a time-charged basis. Wherever possible, Architects should insist that these too are paid for monthly.

Any agreed programme of instalments, whether or not it is based on the examples below, should be referred to in Schedule Three, part 5. There should also be a record of any arrangement agreed for instalments within work stages E–L to be paid in proportion to the value of the services completed or to the value of the works as certified from time to time. Interim payments such as these should be based upon the current budget or the certified cost of the works.

Example 4.1

Fee Instalment Programme for Basic Services (single appointment)

Work stage	% of fees	Cumulative %
C	10	10
D	15	25
E	20	45
FG	20	65
HJKL	33	98
Final Account	2	100

Appointment by stages may be uneconomic but is sometimes unavoidable. Where a project proceeds in fits and starts, is postponed or resumed, or is terminated before completion, the Architect is inevitably faced with additional costs over and above those which can be recovered in the normal way under Conditions 1.5.18–21. Such extras might be in the form of an increased proportion of overheads and/or familiarisation costs.

By applying the instalment programme in the example below, which assumes that an overall percentage fee is negotiated in the usual way, additional costs of this kind will be recovered to some extent at least.

Example 4.2

Fee Instalment Programme for Basic Services (appointment by stages)

Work stage	% of fees	Cumulative %
C	12	12
D	18	30
E	25	55
FG	25	80
HJKL	35	118
Final Account	2	120

The SFA/92 Documents: Worked Examples

Description of Example Project

The commission on which the worked examples of the SFA forms is based concerns a German client who wishes to establish an assembly and supply base in the United Kingdom. The financial incentives of EC development grants make the north of England an attractive location. Acting on recommendations obtained from the RIBA Clients' Advisory Service, and after visiting buildings designed by the three shortlisted firms, the Client selected the young progressive practice, Lynton Knight Architects (LKA).

Following initial discussions, LKA were asked to undertake a feasibility study to investigate the Client's needs, and to provide options for two sites on offer in Northumbria. This service was undertaken for a lump sum fee on the basis of a letter of preliminary appointment (see the example, below).

As a result of this study, a site at Tynegate Business Park was acquired and the parties are now ready to formalise an appointment for basic services using SFA/92. It is envisaged that the services will cover work stages C to K–L, although these are to be activated on a stage by stage basis. Items included within the respective stages for the basic fee are shown on Schedule Two, and the basis for payment is confirmed in Schedule Three. Progress is dependent on the supply of information by the Client, as identified in Schedule One. Schedule Four carries LKA's recommendations for the appointment of other consultants by the Client.

Schedule Two also shows some additional work to be undertaken. The architects have agreed to provide material for publicity brochures (C.08); to submit the project for statutory approvals (D.15 and E.07) to avoid difficulties of language and distance; and also to submit the necessary information to the ground landlords and funding bodies (F–G.09). It is proposed to let a separate contract for preliminary site works (H.08), and LKA have agreed to administer this (K–L.13). All this work will be on a time-charged basis additional to the percentage fee for the basic services.

Example letter   **Preliminary appointment for feasibility study**

We are writing about the terms of our appointment for this project.

You have asked us to undertake some preliminary services so that the project may proceed. We confirm these as follows:

Feasibility study in connection with two sites under consideration at Tynegate Business Park, Northumbria

It is understood that if you subsequently instruct us to undertake other preliminary services, you will confirm this in writing.

The feasibility study, providing options for sites A and B only, can be undertaken by the date you have indicated provided that we receive from you, by 2 February 1992, all the information scheduled in our letter of 16 December 1991.

This study will be carried out within a lump sum fee of £10,000. Any related further studies which you may instruct during the work on the feasibility study will be charged additionally on a time basis and are not to be regarded as included within the lump sum. However, it is accepted that the lump sum figure quoted is to include all expenses incurred during the feasibility study (travel, materials, production of reports and other communications).

Invoices will be submitted monthly during the period we carry out the study. The final balance is to be paid before the report(s) are handed over. VAT will be charged at the current rate (17.5%) on all our fees and expenses.

Will you please confirm your acceptance of the preliminary appointment set out in this letter by signing the enclosed copy and returning it to us.

Memorandum of Agreement

BETWEEN

Parties   (1)   Heinrich Löffler

of 17 Stuttgartstrasse, Frankfurt, Germany   ('the Client')

(2)   Lynton Knight Architects,

of Swan's Wharf, Docklands, London, UK   ('the Architect')

Recitals   **A**   The Client intends to proceed with:

Proposed new assembly plant, offices and ancillary work

('the Project')

The Project relates to the land and/or buildings at:

Tynegate Business Park, Northumbria, UK

('the Site')

    B   The Client wishes to appoint the Architect for the Project and the Architect has agreed to accept such appointment upon and subject to the terms set out in this Agreement.

It is agreed that: 1   The Client hereby appoints the Architect and the Architect hereby accepts appointment for the Project.

    2   This Appointment is made and accepted on the Conditions of Appointment and Schedules attached hereto.

    3   The Architect shall provide the Services specified in Schedule Two.

    4   The Client shall pay the Architect the fees and expenses and disbursements specified in Schedule Three.

    5   No action or proceedings for any breach of this Agreement shall be commenced against the Architect after the expiry of __TEN__ years from completion of the Architect's Services, or, where the Services specific to building projects Stages K–L are provided by the Architect, from the date of practical completion of the Project.

    6.1   The Architect's liability for loss or damage shall be limited to such sum as the Architect ought reasonably to pay having regard to his responsibility for the same on the basis that all other consultants, Specialists, and the contractor, shall where appointed, be deemed to have provided to the Client contractual undertakings in respect of their services and shall be deemed to have paid to the Client such contribution as may be appropriate having regard to the extent of their responsibility for such loss or damage.

    6.2   The liability of the Architect for any loss or damage arising out of any action or proceedings referred to in clause 5 shall, notwithstanding the provisions of clause 6.1, in any event be limited to a sum not exceeding £ 1,000,000-00 .

    6.3   For the avoidance of doubt the Architect's liability shall never exceed the lower of the sum calculated in accordance with clause 6.1 above and the sum provided for in clause 6.2.

Dated 2 July 19 92

AS WITNESS the hands of the parties the day and year first before written

(the Architect)   _(the Client)_

Memorandum of Agreement

(Alternative version for execution as a Deed under the law of England and Wales)

BETWEEN

Parties   (1) _____

of_____('the Client')

(2) _____

of_____('the Architect')

Recitals   A   The Client intends to proceed with:

_____

_____

_____('the Project')

The Project relates to the land and/or buildings at:

_____

_____('the Site')

B   The Client wishes to appoint the Architect for the Project and the Architect has agreed to accept such appointment upon and subject to the terms set out in this Agreement.

It is agreed that: 1   The Client hereby appoints the Architect and the Architect hereby accepts appointment for the Project.

2   This Appointment is made and accepted on the Conditions of Appointment and Schedules attached hereto.

3   The Architect shall provide the Services specified in Schedule Two.

4   The Client shall pay the Architect the fees and expenses and disbursements specified in Schedule Three.

5   No action or proceedings for any breach of this Agreement shall be commenced against the Architect after the expiry of _____ years from completion of the Architect's Services, or, where the Services specific to building projects Stages K–L are provided by the Architect, from the date of practical completion of the Project.

6.1   The Architect's liability for loss or damage shall be limited to such sum as the Architect ought reasonably to pay having regard to his responsibility for the same on the basis that all other consultants, Specialists, and the contractor, shall where appointed, be deemed to have provided to the Client contractual undertakings in respect of their services and shall be deemed to have paid to the Client such contribution as may be appropriate having regard to the extent of their responsibility for such loss or damage.

6.2   The liability of the Architect for any loss or damage arising out of any action or proceedings referred to in clause 5 shall, notwithstanding the provisions of clause 6.1, in any event be limited to a sum not exceeding £ _____.

6.3   For the avoidance of doubt the Architect's liability shall never exceed the lower of the sum calculated in accordance with clause 6.1 above and the sum provided for in clause 6.2.

Dated _____ 19 _____

continued

Standard Form of Agreement for the Appointment of an Architect (SFA/92)

Sheet 3

Memorandum of Agreement (alternative version) *continued*

IN WITNESS whereof this Agreement was executed as a Deed and delivered on the above date.

Executed on behalf of
the Architect

_____

_____   Witness Name [1]
Partner [3] / Director [2]

_____   _____
Partner [3] / Director [2]   Address

Executed on behalf of
the Client

_____

_____   Witness Name [1]
Director / Sec. [2]

_____   _____
Director / Sec. [2]   Address

Footnotes

[1] Under the law of England and Wales, signatures only need witnessing where the document is executed by an *individual*, not a corporate body.

[2] For a corporate body, the signature of two directors, or one director and the company secretary, is required.

[3] For a partnership, all partners must sign except where one has been designated (by Deed) to be their signatory.

Standard Form of Agreement for the Appointment of an Architect (SFA/92)

Definitions

Where the defined terms are used in the SFA documents they are distinguished by an initial capital letter.

Appointment
The agreement between the Client and the Architect for the Project as set out in the Standard Form of Agreement documents.

Architect
The party specified as Architect in the Memorandum of Agreement.

Budget
The sum the Client proposes to spend on the Project inclusive of:

·   professional fees and expenses
·   disbursements
·   statutory charges
·   the Construction Budget;

but excluding:

·   site acquisition costs
·   client's legal and in-house expenses
·   and any VAT thereon.

Client
The party specified as Client in the Memorandum of Agreement.

Client's Requirements
The objectives which the Client wishes to achieve in the Project including functional requirements, environmental standards, life span, and levels of quality.

Collateral Agreement
An agreement between the Architect and a third party existing in parallel with the agreement between the Architect and the Client. Sometimes known as a collateral warranty or a duty of care agreement.

Construction Budget
The sum the Client proposes to spend on the construction of the Project.

Contract Documents
The documents forming the building contract between the Client and a contractor, usually comprising conditions of contract, drawings, specifications and bills of quantities or schedules of rates.

Lead Consultant
The consultant given the authority and responsibility by the Client to coordinate and integrate the services of the other consultants.

Procurement Method
The method by which the building project is to be achieved, determining:

·   the relations between the Client, the design team and the construction team
·   the methods of financing and management, and
·   the form of construction contract

Project
As specified in the Memorandum of Agreement.

Services
The Services to be provided by the Architect as specified in Schedule Two.

Site
As specified in the Memorandum of Agreement.

Site Staff
Staff appointed by either Architect or Client to provide inspection of the Works on behalf of the Client.

continued

Standard Form of Agreement for the Appointment of an Architect (SFA/92)   *Sheet 4*

Definitions *continued*

Specialist

A person or firm, other than the consultants, appointed to provide expertise, skill and care, involving design, in the supply or manufacture of goods, materials or components or in the construction of parts of the Project.

Timetable

The Timetable for the completion of the Services showing *inter alia* any points and/or dates during the course of the carrying out of the Services at which the Architect shall seek the authority of the Client before proceeding further with the Services.

Total Construction Cost

The cost as certified by the Architect of all Works including site works executed under the Architect's direction and control.

It shall include:

·   the cost of all works designed by consultants and co-ordinated by the Architect irrespective of whether such work is carried out under separate building contracts for which the Architect may not be responsible. The Architect shall be informed of the cost of any such contract;

·   the actual or estimated cost of any work executed which is excluded from the contract and which is otherwise designed by the Architect;

·   the cost of built-in furniture and equipment. Where the cost of any special equipment is excluded from the Total Construction Cost the Architect may charge additionally for work in connection with such items;

·   the cost estimated by the Architect of any material, labour or carriage supplied by a Client who is not the contractor.

It shall exclude:

·   the design fees of any Specialists for work on which otherwise consultants would have been employed. Where such fees are not known the Architect will estimate a reduction from the Total Construction Cost.

Where the Client is the contractor, a statement of the ascertained gross cost of the works may be used in calculating the Total Construction Cost of the Works. In the absence of such a statement the Architect's own estimate shall be used. In both a statement of the ascertained gross cost and an Architect's estimate there shall be included an allowance for the contractor's profit and overheads.

Work Stages

Stages into which the process of designing building projects and administering building contracts may be divided in accordance with the RIBA's model *Plan of Work* for design team operation.

Works

The works to be carried out by the construction contractor as described in the Contract Documents; the place where those works are carried out.

Conditions of Appointment

PART ONE

CONDITIONS COMMON TO ALL COMMISSIONS

1.1 Governing law/interpretation

1.1.1   The application of the Appointment shall be governed by the laws of [England and Wales] [Northern Ireland] [Scotland].
Delete those parts not applicable.

1.1.2   The conditions headings and side notes are for the convenience of the parties to this Agreement only and do not affect its interpretation.

1.1.3   Words denoting the masculine gender include the feminine gender and words denoting natural persons include corporations and firms and shall be construed interchangeably in that manner.

1.2 Architect's obligations

Duty of care   1.2.1   The Architect shall in providing the Services exercise reasonable skill and care in conformity with the normal standards of the Architect's profession.

Architect's authority   1.2.2   The Architect shall act on behalf of the Client in the matters set out or necessarily implied in the Appointment.

1.2.3   The Architect shall at those points and/or dates referred to in the Timetable obtain the authority of the Client before proceeding with the Services.

No alteration to services   1.2.4   The Architect shall make no material alteration to or addition to or omission from the Services without the knowledge and consent of the Client except in case of emergency when the Architect shall inform the Client without delay.

Variations   1.2.5   The Architect shall inform the Client upon its becoming apparent that there is any incompatibility between any of the Client's Requirements; or between the Client's Requirements, the Budget and the Timetable; or any need to vary any part of them.

1.2.6   The Architect shall inform the Client on its becoming apparent that the Services and/or the fees and/or any other part of the Appointment and/or any information or approvals need to be varied. The Architect shall confirm in writing any agreement reached.

1.3 Client's obligations

Client's representative   1.3.1   The Client shall name the person who shall exercise the powers of the Client under the Appointment and through whom all instructions to the Architect shall be given.

Information   1.3.2   The Client shall provide to the Architect the information specified in Schedule One.

1.3.3   The Client shall provide to the Architect such further information as the Architect shall reasonably and necessarily request for the performance of the Services: all such information to be provided free of charge and at such times as shall permit the Architect to comply with the Timetable.

1.3.4   The Client accepts that the Architect will rely on the accuracy, sufficiency and consistency of the information supplied by the Client.

1.3.5   The Client shall advise the Architect of the relative priorities of the Client's Requirements, the Budget and the Timetable and shall inform the Architect of any variations to any of them.

Decisions and approvals   1.3.6   The Client shall give such decisions and approvals as are necessary for the performance of the Services and at such times as to enable the Architect to comply with the Timetable.

Architect does not warrant   1.3.7   The Client acknowledges that the Architect does not warrant the work or products of others nor warrants that the Services will or can be completed in accordance with the Timetable.

1.4 Assignment and sub-contracting

Assignment   1.4.1   Neither the Architect nor the Client shall assign the whole or any part of the benefit or in any way transfer the obligation of the Appointment without the consent in writing of the other.

Sub-contracting   1.4.2   The Architect shall not sub-contract any of the Services without the consent in writing of the Client, which consent shall not be unreasonably withheld.

1.5 Payment

Payment   1.5.1   Payment for the Services shall be calculated, charged and paid as set out in Schedule Three.

Percentage fees   1.5.2   Where it is stated in Schedule Three that fees and/or expenses are payable on a percentage basis, then, unless any other basis has been agreed between the Architect and the Client and confirmed by the Architect to the Client in writing, the fees and/or expenses shall be based on the Total Construction Cost of the Works. On the issue of the final certificate under the building contract the fees and/or expenses shall be recalculated on the actual Total Construction Cost.

1.5.3   The following bases shall be used for the calculation of percentage fees based on the Total Construction Cost until that cost has been ascertained:
· until tenders are obtained – the cost estimate;
· after tenders have been obtained – the lowest acceptable tender;
· after the contract is let – the contract sum.

Revise rates   1.5.4   Unless otherwise stated in Schedule Three, time rates and mileage rates for vehicles shall be revised every twelve months from the date of the Appointment.

Fee variation   1.5.5   Where any change is made to the Architect's Services, the Procurement Method, the Client's Requirements, the Budget, or the Timetable, or where the Architect consents to enter into any Collateral Agreement the form or beneficiary of which had not been agreed by the Architect at the date of the Appointment, the fees specified in Schedule Three shall be varied.

Vary lump sum   1.5.6   Where fees and/or expenses are specified in Schedule Three to be a lump sum, that lump sum shall also be varied in accordance with the provisions of Schedule Three.

Additional fees   1.5.7   Where the Architect is involved in extra work and/or expense for which the Architect is not otherwise remunerated caused by:
· the Clients variations to completed work or services;
· the examination and/or negotiation of notices, applications or claims under a building contract;
· delay or for any other reason beyond the Architect's control;
the Architect shall be entitled to additional fees calculated on a time basis.

1.5.8   Where fees and/or expenses are varied under conditions 1.2.6, 1.5.4, 1.5.5 and/or 1.5.6 or where additional fees are payable under condition 1.5.7, the additional or varied fees and/or expenses shall be stated by the Architect in writing.

Incomplete Services   1.5.9   Where the Architect carries out only part of the Services specified in Schedule Two, fees shall be calculated as described in Schedule Three for:
· completed Work Stage [Schedule Two]
· completed Service [Schedule Two]
· completed part [Timetable, Schedule One]
and for the balance of any of the above the fee shall be on the basis of the Architect's estimate of the percentage of completion.

Expenses and disbursements   1.5.10   The Client shall pay the expenses specified in Schedule Three. Expenses other than those specified shall only be charged with the prior authorisation of the Client.

1.5.11   The Client shall reimburse the Architect as specified in Schedule Three for any disbursements made on the Client's behalf.

As referred to in the Memorandum of Agreement dated **2·7·92** between **LKA** and *(signature)* *(parties to initial)*

Standard Form of Agreement for the Appointment of an Architect (SFA/92)

Worked Examples

Maintain records	1.5.12	The Architect shall maintain records of expenses and of disbursements and shall make these available to the Client on reasonable request.
Instalments	1.5.13	All payments due under the Appointment shall be made by instalments specified in Schedule Three. Where no such basis is specified, payments shall be made monthly on the basis of the Architect's estimate of percentage of completion of the Services.
Payment	1.5.14	Payment shall become due to the Architect on submission of the Architect's account.
No setoff	1.5.15	The Client may not withhold or reduce any sum payable to the Architect under the Appointment by reason of claims or alleged claims against the Architect. All rights of setoff which the Client may otherwise exercise in common law are hereby expressly excluded.
Disputed accounts	1.5.16	If any item or part of an item of any account is disputed or subject to question by the Client, the payment by the Client of the remainder of that account shall not be withheld on those grounds.
Interest on oustanding accounts	1.5.17	Any sums remaining unpaid at the expiry of twenty-eight days from the date of submission of an account shall bear interest thereafter, such interest to accrue from day to day at the rate specified in Schedule Three.
Payment on suspension or termination	1.5.18	On suspension or termination of the Appointment the Architect shall be entitled to, and shall be paid, fees for all Services provided to that time calculated as incomplete Services, and to expenses and disbursements reasonably incurred to that time.
	1.5.19	During any period of suspension the Architect shall be reimbursed by the Client for expenses, disbursements and other costs reasonably incurred as a result of the suspension.
	1.5.20	On the resumption of a suspended Service within six months, fees paid prior to resumption shall be regarded solely as payments on account of the total fee.
	1.5.21	Where the Appointment is suspended or terminated by the Client or suspended or terminated by the Architect on account of a breach of the Appointment by the Client, the Architect shall be paid by the Client for all expenses and other costs necessarily incurred as a result of any suspension and any resumption or termination.
VAT	1.5.22	All fees, expenses and disbursements under the Appointment are exclusive of Value Added Tax. Any Value Added Tax on the Architect's services shall be paid by the Client.
	1.6	**Suspension, resumption and termination**
Services impracticable	1.6.1	The Architect shall give reasonable notice in writing to the Client of any circumstances which make it impracticable for the Architect to carry out any of the Services in accordance with the Timetable.
Suspension	1.6.2	The Client may suspend the performance of any or all of the Services by giving reasonable notice in writing to the Architect.
	1.6.3	In the event of the Client's being in default of payment of any fees, expenses and/or disbursements, the Architect may suspend the performance of any or all of the Services on giving notice in writing to the Client.
Resumption	1.6.4	If the Architect has not been given instructions to resume any suspended Service within six months from the date of suspension, the Architect shall request in writing such instructions. If written instructions have not been received within twenty-eight days of the date of such request the Architect shall have the right to treat the Appointment as terminated.
Termination	1.6.5	The Appointment may be terminated by either party on the expiry of reasonable notice in writing.
Architect's death or incapacity	1.6.6	Should the Architect through death or incapacity be unable to provide the Services, the Appointment shall thereby be terminated.
Accrued rights	1.6.7	Termination of the Appointment shall be without prejudice to the accrued rights and remedies of either party.

	1.7	**Copyright**
Copyright	1.7.1	Copyright in all documents and drawings prepared by the Architect and in any work executed from those documents and drawings shall remain the property of the Architect.
	1.8	**Dispute resolution**
Arbitration	1.8.1	In England and Wales, and subject to the provisions of conditions 1.8.2 and 1.8.3 in Northern Ireland, any difference or dispute arising out of the Appointment shall be referred by either of the parties to arbitration by a person to be agreed between the parties or, failing agreement within fourteen days after either party has given the other a written request to concur in the appointment of an arbitrator, a person to be nominated at the request of either party by the President of the Chartered Institute of Arbitrators provided that in a difference or dispute arising out of the conditions relating to copyright the arbitrator shall, unless otherwise agreed, be an architect.
Scotland	1.8.1S	~~In Scotland, subject to the provisions of conditions~~ 1.8.2 and 1.8.3, any difference or dispute arising out of the Appointment shall be referred to arbitration by a person to be agreed between the parties or, failing agreement within fourteen days after either party has given the other a written request to concur in the appointment of an arbiter, a person to be nominated at the request of either party by the Dean of the Faculty of Advocates, provided that in a difference or dispute arising out of the conditions relating to copyright the ~~arbiter shall, unless otherwise agreed, be an architect.~~ *LKA 2.7.92*
Opinion	1.8.2	In Northern Ireland or Scotland, any difference or dispute arising from the Appointment may be referred respectively to the RSUA or the RIAS for an opinion provided that: · the opinion is sought on a joint statement of undisputed facts; · the parties agree to be bound by the opinion.
Negotiation	1.8.3	In Northern Ireland or Scotland, the parties shall attempt to settle any dispute by negotiation and no procedure shall be commenced under condition 1.8.1 or 1.8.1S until the expiry of twenty-eight days after notification has been given in writing by one to the other of a difference or dispute.
	1.8.4	Nothing herein shall prevent the parties agreeing to settle any difference or dispute arising out of the Appointment without recourse to arbitration.

PART TWO		**CONDITIONS SPECIFIC TO DESIGN OF BUILDING PROJECTS, STAGES A–H**
	2.1	**Architect's obligations**
Architect's authority	2.1.1	The Architect shall, where specified in the Timetable, obtain the authority of the Client before initiating any Work Stage and shall confirm that authority in writing.
Procurement Method	2.1.2	The Architect shall advise on the options for the Procurement Method for the Project.
No alteration to design	2.1.3	The Architect shall make no material alteration, addition to or omission from the approved design without the knowledge and consent of the Client and shall confirm such consent in writing.
	2.2	**Client's obligations**
Statutory requirements	2.2.1	The Client shall instruct the making of applications for planning permission and approval under Building Acts, Regulations and other statutory requirements and applications for consents by freeholders and all others having an interest in the Project and shall pay any statutory charges and any fees, expenses and disbursements in respect of such applications.
	2.2.2	The Client shall have informed the Architect prior to the date of the Appointment whether any third party will acquire or is likely to acquire an interest in the whole or any part of the Project.
Collateral Agreements	2.2.3	The Client shall not require the Architect to enter into any Collateral Agreement with a third party which imposes greater obligations or liabilities on the Architect than does the Appointment.
Procurement Method	2.2.4	The Client shall confirm the Procurement Method for the Project.

Standard Form of Agreement for the Appointment of an Architect (SFA/92)

33

2.3 Copyright

2.3.1 Notwithstanding the provisions of condition 1.7.1, the Client shall be entitled to reproduce the Architect's design by proceeding to execute the Project provided that:
- the entitlement applies only to the Site or part of the Site to which the design relates, and
- the Architect has completed a scheme design or
- has provided detail design and production information, and
- any fees, expenses and disbursements due to the Architect have been paid.

This entitlement shall also apply to the maintenance repair and/or renewal of the Works.

2.3.2 Where the Architect has not completed a scheme design, the Client shall not reproduce the design by proceeding to execute the Project without the consent of the Architect.

2.3.3 Where the Services are limited to making and negotiating planning applications, the Client may not reproduce the Architect's design without the Architect's consent, which consent shall not be unreasonably withheld, and payment of any additional fees.

2.3.4 The Architect shall not be liable for the consequences of any use of any information or designs prepared by the Architect except for the purposes for which they were provided.

PART THREE   **CONDITIONS SPECIFIC TO CONTRACT ADMINISTRATION AND INSPECTION OF THE WORKS STAGES J–L**

3.1 Architect's obligations

Visits to the Works — 3.1.1 The Architect shall in providing the Services specified in stages K and L of Schedule Two make such visits to the Works as the Architect at the date of the Appointment reasonably expected to be necessary. The Architect shall confirm such expectation in writing.

Variations to visits to the Works — 3.1.2 The Architect shall, on its becoming apparent that the expectation of the visits to the Works needs to be varied, inform the Client in writing of his recommendations and any consequential variation in fees.

More frequent visits to the Works — 3.1.3 The Architect shall, where the Client requires more frequent visits to the Works than that specified by the Architect in condition 3.1.1, inform the Client of any consquential variation in fees. The Architect shall confirm in writing any agreement reached.

Alteration to design only in emergency — 3.1.4 The Architect may in an emergency make an alteration, addition or omission without the Client's knowledge and consent but shall inform the Client without delay and shall confirm that in writing. Otherwise the Architect shall make no material alteration or addition to or omission from the approved design during construction without the knowledge and consent of the Client, and the Architect shall confirm such consent in writing.

3.2 Client's obligations

Contractor — 3.2.1 The Client shall employ a contractor under a separate agreement to undertake construction or other works relating to the Project.

Responsibilities of contractor — 3.2.2 The Client shall hold the contractor and not the Architect responsible for the contractor's management and operational methods and for the proper carrying out and completion of the Works and for health and safety provisions on the Site.

Products and materials — 3.2.3 The Client shall hold the contractor and not the Architect responsible for the proper installation and incorporation of all products and materials into the Works.

Collateral Agreements — 3.2.4 The Client shall, where the Architect consents to enter into a Collateral Agreement with a third party in respect of the Project, procure that the contractor is equally bound.

Instructions — 3.2.5 The Client shall only issue instructions to the contractor through the Architect, and the Client shall not hold the Architect responsible for any instructions issued other than through the Architect.

3.3 Site Staff

3.3.1 The Architect shall recommend the appointment of Site Staff to the Client if in his opinion such appointments are necessary to provide the Services specified in K–L 04–08 of Schedule Two.

3.3.2 The Architect shall confirm in writing to the Client the Site Staff to be appointed, their disciplines, the expected duration of their employment, the party to appoint them and the party to pay, and the method of recovery of payment to them.

3.3.3 All Site Staff shall be under the direction and control of the Architect.

PART FOUR   **CONDITIONS SPECIFIC TO APPOINTMENT OF CONSULTANTS AND SPECIALISTS WHERE ARCHITECT IS LEAD CONSULTANT**

4.1 Consultants

Nomination — 4.1.1 The Architect shall identify professional services which require the appointment of consultants. Such consultants may be nominated at any time by either the Client or the Architect subject to acceptance by each party.

Appointment — 4.1.2 The Client shall appoint and pay the nominated consultants.

4.1.3 The consultants to be appointed at the date of the Appointment and the services to be provided by them shall be confirmed in writing by the Architect to the Client.

Collateral Agreements — 4.1.4 The Client shall, where the Architect consents to enter into a Collateral Agreement with a third party in respect of the Project, procure that all consultants are equally bound.

Lead Consultant — 4.1.5 The Client shall appoint and give authority to the Architect as Lead Consultant in relation to all consultants however employed. The Architect shall be the medium of all communication and instruction between the Client and the consultants, coordinate and integrate into the overall design the services of the consultants, require reports from the consultants.

4.1.6 The Client shall procure that the provisions of condition 4.1.5 above are incorporated into the conditions of appointment of all consultants however employed and shall provide a copy of such conditions of appointment to the Architect.

Responsibilities of consultants — 4.1.7 The Client shall hold each consultant however appointed and not the Architect responsible for the competence and performance of the services to be performed by the consultant and for the general inspection of the execution of the work designed by the consultant.

Responsibilities of Architect — 4.1.8 Nothing in this Part shall affect any responsibility of the Architect for issuing instructions under the building contract or for other functions ascribed to the Architect under the building contract in relation to work designed by a consultant.

4.2 Specialists

Nomination — 4.2.1 A Specialist who is to be employed directly by the Client or indirectly through the contractor to design any part of the Works may be nominated by either the Architect or the Client subject to acceptance by each party.

Appointment — 4.2.2 The Specialists to be appointed at the date of the Appointment and the services to be provided by them shall be those confirmed in writing by the Architect to the Client.

Collateral Agreements — 4.2.3 The Client shall, where the Architect consents to enter into a Collateral Agreement with a third party in respect of the Project, procure that all Specialists are equally bound.

Coordination and integration — 4.2.4 The Client shall give the authority to the Architect to coordinate and integrate the services of all Specialists into the overall design and the Architect shall be responsible for such coordination and integration.

Responsibilities of Specialists — 4.2.5 The Client shall hold any Specialist and not the Architect responsible for the products and materials supplied by the Specialist and for the competence, proper execution and performance of the work with which such Specialists are entrusted.

Standard Form of Agreement for the Appointment of an Architect (SFA/92)

Schedule One   Information to be supplied by Client

Part One

All Commissions

The information to be supplied by the Client under Conditions 1.3.2 and 1.3.3 shall specifically include:

Client's Requirements ✓   Budget ✓   Timetable ✓

```
See letter HL/MD/ref. 36/017, dated 3.3.91 and enclosures.
```

Other matters:

```
Information on manufacturing and assembly process as
practised in German plant (translated into English).
```

Part Two

Commissions where Services are specific to the design of Building Projects, Work Stages A–H

Where this Part applies, the further information to be supplied by the Client shall specifically include:

matters relating to the site and any buildings thereon including
- ownership and interests ✓
- boundaries ✓
- easements and restrictive and other covenants ✓
- other legal constraints   `-- diversion of Right of Way`
- ~~planning consents obtained and applied for~~
- ~~measured surveys~~
- ~~explorations~~
- any requirement to conform to client systems/working methods `(see below)`

Further matters relating to Client's Requirements including
- schedule of accommodation   } `Full schedules required`
- general level of quality of specification

Other matters:

```
. Manufacturers' literature and drawings of machines and
  other plant systems -- to show fixing details
. Manufacturers' information on computerised warehouse
  racking systems
. Details of the panelling to be imported and reused in
  Board Room
```

Part Three

Commissions where Services are specific to Contract Administration and Inspection of the Works, Work Stages J–L

Where this Part applies, information to be supplied by the Client shall specifically include:

```
. Company logo for site board
. Hospitality requirements and arrangements for publicity
  event near completion
. Staff training and induction prior to handover
```

As referred to in the Memorandum of Agreement dated 2.7.92 between *LKA* and *(signature)* (*parties to initial*)

Schedule Two   Services to be provided by Architect

1 Design Skills	2 Consultancy Services	3 Buildings / Sites	(4) All Commissions
1.01 Provide interior design services	2.01 Provide services as a consultant Architect on a regular or intermittent basis	3.01 Advise on the suitability and selection of sites	(4.01) Obtain the Client's Requirements, Budget and Timetable
1.02 Advise on the selection of furniture and fittings	2.02 Consult statutory authorities	3.02 Make measured surveys, take levels and prepare plans of sites	(4.02) Advise on the need for and the scope of consultants' services and the conditions of their appointment
1.03 Design furniture and fittings	2.03 Provide information in connection with local authority, government and other grants	3.03 Arrange for investigations of soil conditions of sites	4.03 Arrange for and assist in the selection of other consultants
1.04 Inspect the making up of furnishings	2.04 Make applications for local authority, government and other grants	3.04 Advise on the suitability and selection of buildings	
1.05 Advise on works of special quality, e.g. shopfittings	2.05 Conduct negotiations for local authority, government and other grants	3.05 Make measured surveys and prepare drawings of existing buildings	
1.06 Prepare information for installation of works of special quality	2.06 Make submissions to RFAC, UK heritage bodies and/or non-statutory bodies	3.06 Inspect and prepare report and schedule of condition of existing buildings	
1.07 Inspect installation of works of special quality	2.07 Provide information to advisory bodies	3.07 Inspect and prepare report and schedule of dilapidations	
1.08 Advise on commissioning or selection of works of art	2.08 Negotiate with advisory bodies	3.08 Prepare estimates for the replacement and reinstatement of buildings and plant	
1.09 Prepare information for installation of works of art	2.09 Advise on rights including easements and responsibilities of owners and lessees	3.09 Prepare, submit, negotiate claims following damage by fire and other causes	
1.10 Inspect installation of works of art	2.10 Provide information on rights including easements and responsibilities of owners and lessees	3.10 Investigate and advise on means of escape in existing buildings	
1.11 Provide industrial design services	2.11 Negotiate rights including easements	3.11 Investigate and advise on change of use in existing buildings	
1.12 Develop a building system or components for mass production	2.12 Provide services in connection with party wall negotiations	3.12 Investigate and report on building failures	
1.13 Examine and advise on existing building systems	2.13 Provide services in connection with planning appeals and/or inquiries	3.13 Arrange for and inspect exploratory work by contractors and specialists in connection with building failures	
1.14 Monitor testing of prototypes, mock-ups or models of building systems	2.14 Advise on the use of energy in new or existing buildings	3.14 Prepare a layout for the development of a site	
1.15 Provide town planning and urban design services	2.15 Carry out life cycle analyses of proposed or existing buildings to determine their likely cost in use	3.15 Prepare a layout for a greater area than that which is to be developed immediately	
1.16 Provide landscape design services	2.16 Provide services in connection with environmental studies	3.16 Prepare development plans for a site or a large building or a complex of buildings	
1.17 Provide graphic design services	2.17 *deleted*	3.17 Prepare drawings and specifications of materials for the construction of estate roads and sewers	
1.18 Provide exhibition design services	2.18 Prepare, settle proofs, attend conferences and give evidence		
1.19 Provide presentation material design services	2.19 Act as witness as to fact	3.18 Make structural surveys and report on the structural elements of buildings	3.21 Investigate and advise on fire protection and alarms in existing buildings
1.20 Provide perspective and other illustrations	2.20 Act as expert witness	3.19 Investigate and advise on floor loadings in existing buildings	3.22 Investigate and advise on security systems in existing buildings
1.21 Provide model-making services	2.21 Act as arbitrator	3.20 Investigate and advise on sound insulation in existing buildings	3.23 Inspect and prepare a valuation report for mortgage or other purpose
1.22 Provide photographic record services	2.22 Provide project management services		
1.23	2.23		3.24 ....

As referred to in the Memorandum of Agreement dated **2·7·92** between **JKA** and **[initials]** *(parties to initial)*

Schedule Two   Services specific to Building Projects

Stages

A–B Inception and Feasibility	 C Outline Proposals	D Scheme Design	E Detail Design
01 Obtain information about the Site from the Client	01 Analyse the Client's Requirements; prepare outline proposals	01 Develop scheme design from approved outline proposals	01 Develop detail design from approved scheme design
02 Visit the Site and carry out an initial appraisal	02 Provide information to discuss proposals with and incorporate input of other consultants	02 Provide information to, discuss proposals with and incorporate input of other consultants into scheme design	02 Provide information to, discuss proposals with and incorporate input of other consultants into detail design
03 Assist the Client in preparation of Client's Requirements	03 Provide information to other consultants for their preparation of an approximation of construction cost	03 Provide information to other consultants for their preparation of cost estimate	03 Provide information to other consultants for their revision of cost estimate
04 Advise the Client on methods of procuring construction	03A Prepare an ~~approximation of construction cost~~	03A Prepare ~~cost estimate~~	03A Revi~~se cost~~ estimate
05 Advise on the need for specialist contractors, sub-contractors and suppliers to design and execute parts of the Works	04 Submit outline proposals and approximation of construction cost for the Client's preliminary approval	04 Prepare preliminary timetable for construction	04 Prepare applications for approvals under Building Acts and/or Regulations and other statutory requirements
06 Prepare proposals and make application for outline planning permission	05 Propose a procedure for cost planning and control	05 Consult with planning authorities	04A Prepare buildi~~ng notice~~ under Buildi~~ng Acts~~ and/or ~~Re~~gulations
07 Carry out such studies as may be necessary to determine the feasibility of the Client's Requirements	06 Provide information to others for cost planning and control throughout the Project	06 Consult with building control authorities	05 Agree form of building contract and explain the Client's obligations thereunder
08 Review with the Client alternative design and construction approaches and cost implications	06A Operate the procedure for cost planning and control throughout the Project	07 Consult with fire authorities	06 Obtain the Client's approval of the type of construction, quality of materials and standard of workmanship
09 Advise on the need to obtain planning permission, approvals under Building Acts and/or Regulations and other statutory requirements	07 Prepare and keep updated a Client's running expenditure plan for the Project	08 Consult with environmental authorities	(07) Apply for approvals under Building Acts and/or Regulations and other statutory requirements
10 Develop the Client's Requirements	(08) Prepare special presentation drawings, brochures, models or technical information for use of the Client or others	09 Consult with licensing authorities	07A Give building notice under Building Acts and/or Regulations
11 Advise on environmental impact and prepare report	09 Carry out negotiations with tenants or others identified by the Client	10 Consult with statutory undertakers	08 Negotiate if necessary over Building Acts and/or Regulations and other statutory requirements and revise production information
12	10	11 Prepare an application for full planning permission	09 Conduct exceptional negotiations for approvals by statutory authorities
		12 Submit scheme design showing spatial arrangements, materials and appearance, together with cost estimate, for the Client's approval	10 Negotiate waivers or relaxations under Building Acts and/or Regulations and other statutory requirements
		13 Consult with tenants or others identified by the Client	11 ....
		14 Conduct exceptional negotiations with planning authorities	
		(15) Submit an application for full planning permission	
		16 Prepare multiple applications for full planning permission	
		17 Submit multiple applications for full planning permission	
		18 Make revisions to scheme design to deal with requirements of planning authorities	
		19 Revise planning application	
		20 Resubmit planning application	
		21 Carry out special constructional research for the Project including design of prototypes, mock-ups or models	
		22 Monitor testing of prototypes, mock-ups or models etc.	
		23	

Work Stages
are specified by circling the stage letters.

Basic Services
indicated by the ~~coloured~~ area are specified unless struck out.   *boxed*

Additional Services
are specified by circling the relevant numbered items.

Schedule Two   Services specific to Building Projects

Stages

F–G Production Information and Bills of Quantities	**H** Tender Action	**J** Project Planning	**K–L** Operations on Site and Completion
01 Prepare production drawings	01 Advise on and obtain the Client's approval to a list of tenderers for the building contract	01 Advise the Client on the appointment of the contractor and on the responsibilities of the parties and the Architect under the building contract	01 Administer the terms of the building contract
02 Prepare specification	02 Invite tenders	02 Prepare the building contract and arrange for it to be signed	02 Conduct meetings with the contractor to review progress
03 Provide information for the preparation of bills of quantities and/or schedules of works	03 Appraise and report on tenders with other consultants	03 Provide production information as required by the building contract	03 Provide information to other consultants for the preparation of financial reports to the Client
03A Prepare schedules of rates and/or quantities and/or schedules of works for tendering purposes	03A* Appraise and report on tenders	04 Provide services in connection with demolitions	03A Prepare financial reports for the Client
04 Provide information to, discuss proposals with and incorporate input of other consultants into production information	04 Assist other consultants in negotiating with a tenderer	05 Arrange for other contracts to be let subsequent to the commencement of the building contract	04 Generally inspect materials delivered to the site
	04A Negotiate with a tenderer	06	05 As appropriate instruct sample taking and carrying out tests of materials, components, techniques and workmanship and examine the conduct and results of such tests whether on or off site
05 Co-ordinate production information	05 Assist other consultants in negotiating a price with a contractor		
06 Provide information to other consultants for their revision of cost estimate	05A Negotiate a price with a contractor		06 As appropriate instruct the opening up of completed work to determine that it is generally in accordance with the Contract Documents
06A Revise cost estimate	06 Select a contractor by other means		
07 Review timetable for construction	07 Revise production information to adjust tender sum		07 As appropriate visit the sites of the extraction and fabrication and assembly of materials and components to inspect such materials and workmanship before delivery to site
08 Prepare other production information	08 Arrange for other contracts to be let prior to the main building contract		
09 Submit plans for proposed building works for approval of landlords, funders, freeholders, tenants or others as requested by the Client	09		08 At intervals appropriate to the stage of construction visit the Works to inspect the progress and quality of the Works and to determine that they are being executed generally in accordance with the Contract Documents
10			09 Direct and control the activities of Site Staff
			10 Provide drawings showing the building and the main lines of drainage
			11 Arrange for drawings of building services installations to be provided
			12 Give general advice on maintenance
			13 Administer the terms of other contracts
			14 Monitor the progress of the Works against the contractor's programme and report to the Client
		19 Incorporate information prepared by others in maintenance manuals	15 Prepare valuations of work carried out and completed
		20 Prepare a programme for the maintenance of a building	16 Provide specially prepared drawings of a building as built
		21 Arrange maintenance contracts	17 Prepare drawings for conveyancing purposes
		22	18 Compile maintenance and operational manuals

Schedule Three   Fees and Expenses

VAT, where applicable, is charged on all fees and expenses

---

1 Fees

. Basic Services for Stages C to K--L inclusive, as shown on Schedule Two (basis as Condition 1.5.2), Fee 5.5%
. Services C.08, D.15, E.07, F--G.09, H.08, K--L.13 and 14 on a time basis (see (2) below).

---

2 Time rates

The rates for Services to be charged on a time basis shall be calculated as follows:

. Principals at £500 per day
. Technical staff at £35 per hour (average)

Time rates shall be revised each year on: 1 January

---

3 Expenses

The following expenses shall be charged by the Architect:

. Cost of producing necessary documents
. Postage, telephone, fax, courier services
. Three visits to Frankfurt for two persons (economy class), hotel charges and subsistence
(Photography, model-making and publicity material to be disbursements)

		Mileage rates where applicable shall be:
● at cost	_____	40p_____
● cost plus	_____15_%	and shall be revised each year on:
● a lump sum of	£_____	1 January
● an additional % fee of	_____%	

---

4 Disbursements

For disbursements made under condition 1.5.11 the Architect shall charge:

● at cost plus   _____20_%   ● other   _____

---

5 Instalments

Fees and expenses shall be paid by instalments in accordance with the following programme:

Interim payments monthly, on last day of month, of £15,000, subject to the following stage payments:
. submission of scheme design (D) -- 35%
. on issue of invitations to tender (H) -- 75%
Time rates: monthly, on the last day of each month.
Expenses and disbursements: monthly, on the last day of the month following invoice.

---

6 Site Staff

For Site Staff (under Conditions 3.3.1 and 3.3.2) appointed and paid by the Architect, the Architect shall be reimbursed as follows:

● on a Time Basis, or   £150 per day
_____
● on Annual Salary Cost plus:_____% (salaries to be stated, where appropriate)

---

7 Interest on overdue accounts

The interest rate payable under condition 1.5.17 shall be: ● either_____%

● or_____3%_____% over   Royal Bank
of Scotland   (measure of base rate)

As referred to in the Memorandum of Agreement dated *2.7.92* between *LKA*   and *(signature)* *(parties to initial)*

Schedule Four   Appointment of Consultants, Specialists and Site Staff

Consultants   (under Conditions 4.1.2 and 4.1.3)

Services*	Name, address *(where known)*
Quantity surveying	Mason Clerk Partnership, 254 John Street, Manchester
Structural engineering	Crimp & Speedweld, 6 Coldacre, Oldham
M. & E. engineering	A. & D.C. Short, 27 Jubilee Road, Sunderland

Specialists   (under Condition 4.2.2)

Services*	Name, address *(where known)*	To be appointed (a) directly by Client (b) indirectly by Contractor
Canteen & catering equipment	Max Braun, Friedrichstrasse 1528, Dusseldorf	(a)
Lifts & automated ramps	Wolf & Becker, 12 Weirside, North Shields	(b)

*Extent of services to be defined in appointing letter or other document – to be copied to the Architect.

Site Staff   (under Condition 3.3.2)

Description	Duration	No. of staff	By whom appointed and paid
Private clerk of works	Intermittently as directed by Architect	One	Architect

As referred to in the Memorandum of Agreement dated 2.7.92 between LKA and (*parties to initial*)

Standard Form of Agreement for the Appointment of an Architect (SFA/92)   Sheet 8

Alternative / Supplementary Schedules of Services

Community Architecture (supplementary schedule)

Supplementary Schedule of Services for Community Architecture Projects

---

Standard Form of Agreement for the
Appointment of an Architect (SFA/92)

Community Architecture

Supplementary Schedule of Services

Royal Institute of British Architects
Royal Incorporation of Architects in Scotland
Royal Society of Ulster Architects
Association of Consultant Architects

To be used in conjunction with the standard Schedule Two of the *Standard Form of Agreement for the Appointment of an Architect* (SFA/92).

NOTES ON USE AND COMPLETION

Community Architecture services apply where the intended user, or users, is able to play a full part as User Client in the design process and, sometimes, in the building process. The User Client may or may not be the Client who is financing the Project. The Architect may be employed to act as 'enabler' in matters of organisation, promotion and fund-raising. The User Client is frequently a group of people, and the Architect may be employed to coordinate input from the group into the design and building processes.

The scope and extent of Community Architecture (CA) services can seldom be defined precisely at the outset, and for this reason services will be normally be charged on a time basis, although for some services an agreed lump sum will be appropriate. While most services will concern the inception and feasibility stages, some will relate to design and construction.

Some of the services set out in the Supplementary Schedule will be relevant to spheres of work other than those under a Community Architecture banner, particularly in the housing field.

The Supplementary Schedule

Conditions of Appointment

Two additional Definitions are given: for Community Architecture itself, and for the 'User Client'.

In CA projects it is essential to distinguish between 'the Client', as defined in the *Standard Form of Agreement for the Appointment of an Architect*, and the User Client, ie the intended user of the Project, who plays a critical role throughout its design and construction and who may or may not be the Client. To clarify this distinction, there are additional Conditions of Appointment which apply where the User Client is not the Client. These are intended to overcome any problems arising in connection with lines of communication and/or authority.

Because the nature of CA work makes it difficult to predict with certainty at the outset the scope and cost of the services to be provided, it is essential for the parties to maintain systematic administrative procedures and confirm agreed additions/amendments to the Services promptly and accurately.

Completion

To incorporate the Supplementary Schedule into the *Standard Form of Agreement for the Appointment of an Architect* it is necessary to make an addition to the Memorandum of Agreement at the third clause. This should read.

3   The Architect shall provide the Services specified in Schedule Two and the Supplementary Schedule of Services for Community Architecture Projects.

On the Supplementary Schedule, ring round the numbers of the services required; insert the name of the User Client or Clients in the space provided; and make sure that the Schedule is dated and initialled at the foot of the page.

Complete the other Schedules in the SFA as appropriate, setting out clearly in Schedule Three the basis for charging fees and expenses.

On the inside front cover of the SFA, tick the documents being used in this appointment.

Further information

Further information on Community Architecture services may be obtained from the Community Architecture Resource Centre, RIBA, 66 Portland Place, London W1N 4AD (tel: 071-580 5533).

Supplementary Schedule of Services for Community Architecture Projects

This Schedule sets out the additional services which may be provided by the Architect for a Community Architecture (CA) project to augment the standard services set out in Schedule Two of the *Standard Form of Agreement for the Appointment of an Architect.* The list of services is not exhaustive, and not all of them will be required on every project. Each service is prefixed by the letters CA.

Services
are specified by circling the relevant numbered items.

COMMUNITY DEVELOPMENT

CA1.0 Assist the User Client to develop and organise as a group.

1.1 Attend group meetings.

1.2 Advise on and assist with constitutional and management matters.

1.3 Carry out social surveys and/or social appraisals.

1.4 Set up and maintain a project office accessible to the User Client.

PROJECT EDUCATION

CA2.0 Acquaint the User Client with the design and building processes.

2.1 Develop design and planning aids for User Client participation.

2.2 Assist the User Client in choosing an appropriate building and/or site.

2.3 Establish contact with relevant people, projects and information sources to assist the User Client.

FEASIBILITY STUDIES

CA3.0 Provide resources and skills additional to those set out in Schedule Two of the *Standard Form of Agreement for the Appointment of an Architect*, work stages A–B.

3.1 Assist the User Client to argue a case for capital and/or revenue funding.

3.2 Prepare business viability plans.

LAY COMMUNICATION

CA4.0 Produce information specifically for communication with the User Client.

4.1 Prepare and distribute drawings, models, programmes, newsletters and questionnaires.

USER CLIENT MEETINGS

CA5.0 Assist the User Client to participate in the design and building processes.

5.1 Organise and attend meetings between User Client and funding bodies, and other special meetings.

5.2 Organise and attend regular strategy and/or steering group meetings.

SPECIAL NEGOTIATIONS

CA6.0 Assist the User Client in obtaining project sponsorship.

6.1 Prepare project sponsorship packs and/or displays.

6.2 Make presentations to funding bodies and other sponsors.

6.3 Complete grant and sponsorship applications.

CUSTOMISATION

CA7.0 Provide for individual customisation within larger projects in collaboration with individual User Clients or groups.

ALTERNATIVE CONTRACTUAL METHODS

CA8.0 Provide additional Services and/or prepare additional information as a result of alternative procurement and contractual methods such as self-build projects and projects involving semi-skilled labour or self-help.

OPERATIONS ON SITE

CA9.0 Acquaint the User Client with works on site.

9.1 Organise individual and group site visits/briefings.

9.2 Involve the User Client in site and progress meetings.

9.3 Set up and operate User Client site offices.

SPECIAL REPORTS

CA10.0 Prepare information where funding bodies and other sponsors have criteria requiring special compliance procedures.

10.1 Prepare special reports as necessary.

10.2 Prepare reports to meet unforeseen events and circumstances.

MANAGEMENT AND MAINTENANCE INFORMATION

CA11.0 Prepare information for the User Client on management and maintenance.

11.1 Advise the User Client on alternative structures for management of buildings and assist with implementation.

11.2 Provide post-completion advice on monitoring, updating and revising management information and maintenance procedures.

CA12.0 ....

....

User Client

Name of User Client or Clients

....

....

....

As referred to in the Memorandum of Agreement dated   between   and   *(parties to initial)*

Supplementary Schedule of Services for Community Architecture Projects

Additional Definitions

Community Architecture
The regeneration and improvement of environmental, economic and employment conditions in both urban and rural areas by committed local people working together with sympathetic professionals of various disciplines.

User Client
The individual, individuals or group of individuals recognised by the Client as the intended User Client or Clients of the Project.

Additional Conditions of Appointment

CONDITIONS SPECIFIC TO PROJECTS WHERE THE USER CLIENT IS NOT THE CLIENT

1.2.2 *(a)* The Architect shall inform the Client of all requests from the User Client for information and/or Services and of any effect of such requests on fees, and shall confirm in writing any agreement reached.

1.2.2 *(b)* The Architect shall not accept or act on any instruction from the User Client without the authority of the Client, and shall confirm such authority in writing.

1.2.2 *(c)* The Architect shall inform the Client of any information provided to the Architect by the User Client.

1.3.1 *(a)* The Client shall name the User Client.

1.3.1 *(b)* The Client shall confirm to the Architect any instruction from the User Client which is to be treated as an instruction from the Client.

1.3.2 *(a)* The Client shall be responsible for all information provided to the Architect by the User Client.

Historic Buildings (alternative schedule)

Alternative Schedule of Services for
Historic Buildings: Repairs and Conservation Work

Standard Form of Agreement for the
Appointment of an Architect (SFA 6/92)

Historic Buildings:
Repairs and Conservation Work

Alternative Schedule of Services

Royal Institute of British Architects
Royal Incorporation of Architects in Scotland
Royal Society of Ulster Architects
Association of Consultant Architects

This Schedule replaces Schedule Two in the *Standard Form of Agreement for the Appointment of an Architect* (SFA/92).

NOTES ON USE AND COMPLETION

This alternative schedule is intended for use where the architect's services are provided in connection with the repair or conservation of an historic building. The work may involve alterations to the building as well as repair of the fabric, and its degree of complexity can vary considerably. For that reason, no complement of 'basic services' is indicated in the schedule. The work typically requires more decision-making on site as work proceeds than is normal for other types of building work; therefore it is the nature of the work rather than the class of building that will determine the scope of the architect's services.

'Historic building'
For the purposes of this document, an historic building is defined as a building, monument or structure of architectural, historical or archaeological interest. Some are protected by legislation and are categorised by various descriptions, such as 'Listed Building', 'Scheduled Monument', 'Ancient Monument', and as buildings in 'conservation areas'. Others may warrant the same special care and attention because of their inherent artistic character or age.

'Conservation'
Sir Bernard Feilden, in his book, *Conservation of Historic Buildings* (1982), defines conservation as the action taken to prevent decay. 'It embraces all acts that prolong the life of our cultural and natural heritage,' he says, the object being to present to those who use and look at historic buildings with wonder the artistic and human messages that such buildings possess.'

'Conservator'
The description 'conservator' is included wherever there is reference to consultancy services in the alternative schedule, and the term may need explanation. A broad definition of a conservator is a consultant or craftsman who specialises in the maintenance, repair or consolidation of works of art such as sculpture, metalwork, stained glass or wall paintings.

The Alternative Schedule of Services

Conditions of Appointment   The alternative schedule replaces the standard Schedule Two in the set of SFA documents. The standard schedule should be discarded. The Conditions printed on the reverse of the alternative schedule are the same as those printed on the reverse of the standard form: no terms or phrases specific to conservation work have been added or incorporated.

Lists of Services   The lists of services are significantly different from those set out in the standard Schedule Two to reflect the nature and complexity of conservation work and the need for expert knowledge and skills in many aspects of it. In particular, the arrangement of work stages A–D differs from the arrangement under the RIBA's model *Plan of Work*.

No complement of basic services is indicated, and the services required should be individually selected. Part 4 of the list of general services applies to all commissions and includes reference to conservators. Under 5 (Special Services) there is a group of services relating to historical research, the making of archaeological records following opening up, and the completion of preliminary applications to grant-aiding authorities.

Completion   To incorporate the alternative schedule into the *Standard Form of Agreement for the Appointment of an Architect* it is necessary to amend the Memorandum of Agreement at the third clause to read:

3   The Architect shall provide the Services specified in the Schedule of Services for Historic Buildings: Repairs and Conservation Work.

On the alternative Schedule Two, circle the services required under the relevant work stages. Make sure that the Schedule is dated and initialled at the foot of the page.

Complete the other Schedules in the SFA as appropriate, setting out clearly in Schedule Three the basis for charging fees and expenses. Where the appointment of conservators is recommended, the details (if known at this early stage) can be set out in Schedule Four.

Refer to the checklist on the inside front cover of the SFA, and tick the documents being used in this appointment.

© 1992 RIBA/RIAS/RSUA/ACA   7.92   C B A   *Standard Form of Agreement for the Appointment of an Architect (SFA/92)*

*Alternative Schedule Two**

Services to be provided by Architect
Historic Buildings: Repairs and Conservation Work

1 **Design Skills**	2 **Consultancy Services**	3 **Buildings / Sites**	4 **All Commissions**
1.01 Provide interior design services	2.01 Provide services as a consultant Architect on a regular or intermittent basis	3.01 Advise on the suitability and selection of sites	(4.01) Discuss the Client's Requirements, Budget and Timetable; assess these and give general guidance on how to proceed
1.02 Advise on the selection of furniture and fittings	2.02 Consult statutory authorities	3.02 Make measured surveys, take levels and prepare plans of sites	(4.02) Advise on the need for and the scope of consultants' and conservators' services and the conditions of their appointment
1.03 Design furniture and fittings	2.03 Provide information in connection with local authority, government and other grants	3.03 Arrange for investigations of soil conditions of sites	4.03 Arrange for and assist in the selection of other consultants and conservators
1.04 Inspect the making up of furnishings		3.04 Advise on the suitability and selection of buildings	
1.05 Advise on works of special quality, e.g. shopfittings	2.04 Make applications for local authority, government and other grants	3.05 Make measured surveys and prepare drawings of existing buildings	
1.06 Prepare information for installation of works of special quality	2.05 Conduct negotiations for local authority, government and other grants	3.06 Inspect and prepare report and schedule of condition of existing buildings	
1.07 Inspect installation of works of special quality	2.06 Make submissions to RFAC, UK heritage bodies and/or non-statutory bodies	3.07 Inspect and prepare report and schedule of dilapidations	**5 Special Services**
1.08 Advise on commissioning or selection of works of art	2.07 Provide information to advisory bodies	3.08 Prepare estimates for the replacement and reinstatement of buildings and plant	5.01 Carry out and coordinate historical research into the building, its structure, fabric and finishes, and its surroundings
1.09 Prepare information for installation of works of art	2.08 Negotiate with advisory bodies	3.09 Prepare, submit, negotiate claims following damage by fire and other causes	5.02 Undertake investigative analyses and record results
1.10 Inspect installation of works of art	2.09 Advise on rights including easements and responsibilities of owners and lessees	3.10 Investigate and advise on means of escape in existing buildings	5.03 Record details of the work as opened up by means of sketches, measured drawings or photographs as appropriate prior to repair in order to provide an archaeological record if required by the Client and/or such bodies as English Heritage or local authorities
1.11 Provide industrial design services	2.10 Provide information on rights including easements and responsibilities of owners and lessees	3.11 Investigate and advise on change of use in existing buildings	
1.12 Develop a building system or components for mass production	2.11 Negotiate rights including easements	3.12 Investigate and report on building failures	5.04 Carry out work to meet the requirements of a grant-aiding authority
1.13 Examine and advise on existing building systems	2.12 Provide services in connection with party wall negotiations	3.13 Arrange for and inspect exploratory work by contractors and specialists in connection with building failures	5.05 Prepare reports, financial information, and complete or advise on the completion of forms supporting claims for payment of grants with valuations and certificates
1.14 Monitor testing of prototypes, mock-ups or models of building systems	2.13 Provide services in connection with planning appeals and/or inquiries		
1.15 Provide town planning and urban design services	2.14 Advise on the use of energy in new or existing buildings	3.14 Prepare a layout for the development of a site	
1.16 Provide landscape design services	2.15 Carry out life cycle analyses of proposed or existing buildings to determine their likely cost in use	3.15 Prepare a layout for a greater area than that which is to be developed immediately	
1.17 Provide graphic design services		3.16 Prepare development plans for a site or a large building or a complex of buildings	
1.18 Provide exhibition design services	2.16 Provide services in connection with environmental studies	3.17 Prepare drawings and specifications of materials for the construction of estate roads and sewers	
1.19 Provide presentation material design services	2.17 *deleted*		
1.20 Provide perspective and other illustrations	2.18 Prepare, settle proofs, attend conferences and give evidence	3.18 Make structural surveys and report on the structural elements of buildings	**3 *continued***
1.21 Provide model-making services	2.19 Act as witness as to fact	3.19 Investigate and advise on floor loadings in existing buildings	3.21 Investigate and advise on fire protection and alarms in existing buildings
1.22 Provide photographic record services	2.20 Act as expert witness		3.22 Investigate and advise on security systems in existing buildings
1.23	2.21 Act as arbitrator	3.20 Investigate and advise on sound insulation in existing buildings	3.23 Inspect and prepare a valuation report for mortgage or other purpose
	2.22 Provide project management services		
* This Schedule replaces Schedule Two of the *Standard Form of Agreement for the Appointment of an Architect*	2.23		3.24 ....

As referred to in the Memorandum of Agreement dated   between   and   *(parties to initial)*

Alternative Schedule Two

Services specific to Building Projects – Historic Buildings

Stages ✱

A	Initial Briefing and Appraisal	B	Detailed Inspection and Report	C	Outline Proposals	D	Detailed Proposals and Statutory Consents
01	Obtain information about the Site or building from the Client	01	Advise on the need for, and extent of opening up of the fabric	01	Analyse the Client's Requirements; prepare outline proposals for the Client's approval	01	Develop detailed proposals from approved outline proposals
02	Visit the Site and carry out an initial appraisal	02	Advise on the need for providing additional access by way of ladders, hoists etc.	02	Provide information to discuss proposals with and incorporate input of other consultants and conservators	02	Provide information to, discuss proposals with and incorporate input of other consultants and conservators into detailed proposals
03	Assist the Client in the preparation of Client's Requirements	03	Advise on and arrange for the appointment of contractors for any opening up	03	Provide information to other consultants and conservators for their preparation of an approximation of construction cost	03	Provide information to other consultants and conservators for their preparation of cost estimate
04	Advise the Client on methods of procuring construction	04	Direct contractors during any opening up	03A	Prepare an approximation of construction cost	03A	Prepare cost estimate
05	Advise on the need for specialist contractors, sub-contractors and suppliers to design and execute parts of the Works	05	Research archival material	04	Propose a procedure for cost planning and control	04	Prepare preliminary timetable for construction
06	Prepare proposals and make application for outline planning permission	06	Undertake a detailed inspection of the property and provide a written report on the findings relating to the condition of the fabric; the feasibility of alterations; recommendations for repair and their order of priority	05	Provide information to others for cost planning and control throughout the Project	05	Consult with planning authorities
07	Carry out such studies as may be necessary to determine the feasibility of the Client's Requirements	07	Make measured surveys, take levels and prepare plans of sites and buildings	05A	Operate the procedure for cost planning and control throughout the Project	06	Consult with building control authorities
08	Review with the Client alternative design and construction approaches and cost implications	08	Brief other consultants and/or conservators; coordinate their initial investigation work; and integrate their recommendations into the overall report on the fabric	06	Prepare and keep updated a Client's running expenditure plan for the Project	07	Consult with fire authorities
09	Advise on the need to obtain planning permission, approvals under Building Acts and/or Regulations and other statutory requirements	09	Submit detailed report to the Client	07	Prepare special presentation drawings, brochures, models or technical information for use of the Client or others	08	Consult with environmental authorities
10	Develop the Client's Requirements	10	....	08	Carry out negotiations with tenants or others identified by the Client	09	Consult with licensing authorities
11	Advise on environmental impact and prepare report			09	Submit outline proposals and an approximation of construction cost for the Client's preliminary approval	10	Consult with statutory undertakers
12	Advise on funding and the possibilities of obtaining grant aid			10	....	11	Prepare an application for full planning permission
13	Submit a preliminary report and recommendations to the Client					12	Make application for listed building consent
14	....					13	Make application for conservation area consent
						14	Consult with tenants or others identified by the Client
						15	Conduct exceptional negotiations with planning authorities
						16	Submit an application for full planning permission
						17	Prepare multiple applications for full planning permission
						18	Submit multiple applications for full planning permission
						19	Make revisions to scheme design to deal with requirements of planning authorities
						20	Revise planning application
						21	Resubmit planning application

✱ Note that the arrangement of work stages A–D differs from the model *Plan of Work*.

D	*continued*
24	Submit scheme design showing spatial arrangements, materials and appearance, together with cost estimate, for the Client's approval
25	....

22	Carry out special constructional research for the Project including design of prototypes, mock-ups or models
23	Monitor testing of prototypes, mock-ups or models etc.

Work Stages
are specified by circling the stage letters.

Services
All services are specified by circling the relevant numbered items.

Standard Form of Agreement for the Appointment of an Architect (SFA/92)   *Sheet 6(HB)b*

Alternative Schedule Two

Stages

Services specific to Building Projects – Historic Buildings

E Detail Design	F–G Production Information and Bills of Quantities	H Tender Action	K–L Operations on Site and Completion
01 Develop detail design from approved detailed proposals	01 Prepare production drawings	01 Advise on and obtain the Client's approval to a list of tenderers for the building contract	01 Administer the terms of the building contract
02 Provide information to, discuss proposals with, and incorporate input of other consultants and/or conservators into detail design	02 Prepare specification	02 Invite tenders	02 Conduct meetings with the contractor to review progress
	03 Provide information for the preparation of bills of quantities and/or schedules of works	03 Appraise and report on tenders with other consultants and/or conservators	03 Provide information to other consultants and/or conservators for the preparation of financial reports to the Client
03 Provide information to other consultants and/or conservators for their revision of cost estimate	03A Prepare schedule of rates and/or quantities and/or schedules of works for tendering purposes	03A Appraise and report on tenders	03A Prepare financial reports for the Client
03A Revise cost estimate	04 Provide information to, discuss proposals with and incorporate input of other consultants and/or conservators into production information	04 Assist other consultants and/or conservators in negotiating with a tenderer	04 Generally inspect materials delivered to the site
04 Prepare applications for approvals under Building Acts and/or Regulations and other statutory requirements		04A Negotiate with a tenderer	05 As appropriate instruct sample taking and carrying out tests of materials, components, techniques and workmanship, and examine the conduct and results of such tests whether on or off site
04A Prepare building notice under Building Acts and/or Regulations ✱	05 Co-ordinate production information	05 Assist other consultants and/or conservators in negotiating a price with a contractor	
05 Agree form of building contract and explain the Client's obligations thereunder	06 Provide information to other consultants and/or conservators for their revision of cost estimate	05A Negotiate a price with a contractor	06 As appropriate instruct the opening up of completed work to determine that it is generally in accordance with the Contract Documents
06 Apply for approvals under Building Acts and/or Regulations and other statutory requirements	06A Revise cost estimate	06 Select a contractor by other means	07 As appropriate visit the sites of the extraction and fabrication and assembly of materials and components to inspect such materials and workmanship before delivery to site
	07 Review timetable for construction	07 Revise production information to adjust tender sum	
06A Give building notice under Building Acts and/or Regulations ✱	08 Prepare other production information	08 Arrange for other contracts to be let prior to the main building contract	
07 Negotiate if necessary over Building Acts and/or Regulations and other statutory requirements and revise production information	09 Submit plans for proposed building works for approval of landlords, funders, free-holders, tenants or others as requested by the Client	09	08 At intervals appropriate to the stage of construction, visit the Works to inspect the progress and quality of the Works and to determine that they are being executed generally in accordance with the Contract Documents
08 Conduct exceptional negotiations for approvals by statutory authorities	10		09 Provide further information if the work reveals new or unforeseen problems
09 Negotiate waivers or relaxations under Building Acts and/or Regulations and other statutory requirements		**J Project Planning**	10 Direct and control the activities of Site Staff
10 Obtain the Client's approval of the type of construction, quality of materials and standard of workmanship		01 Advise the Client on the appointment of the contractor and on the responsibilities of the parties and the Architect under the building contract	11 Provide drawings showing the building and the main lines of drainage
11		02 Prepare the building contract and arrange for it to be signed	12 Arrange for drawings of building services installations to be provided
		03 Provide production information as required by the building contract	13 Give general advice on maintenance
		04 Provide services in connection with demolitions	14 Administer the terms of other contracts
		05 Arrange for other contracts to be let subsequent to the commencement of the building contract	15 Monitor the progress of the Works against the contractor's programme and report to the Client
		06	16 Prepare valuations of work carried out and completed
		K–L *continued*	17 Provide specially prepared drawings of a building as built
		19 Compile maintenance and operational manuals	18 Prepare drawings for conveyancing purposes
		20 Incorporate information prepared by others in maintenance manuals	
		21 Prepare a programme for the maintenance of a building	
		22 Arrange maintenance contracts	
✱ Not applicable in Scotland		23	

Standard Form of Agreement for the Appointment of an Architect (SFA/92)

Sheet 6(HB)c

The SFA CDM Supplement

Supplement to take account of the Health and Safety
Construction (Design and Management) Regulations 1994

Standard Form of Agreement for the
Appointment of an Architect (SFA/92)

Supplement

to take account of the Health and Safety
Construction (Design and Management)
Regulations 1994

Issued April 1995

Royal Institute of British Architects

To be used in conjunction with the Standard Form of Agreement for the Appointment of an
Architect (SFA/92), with or without the Community Architecture supplement or the Historic
Buildings alternative. Also for use with the SFA Design and Build documents, both versions
(Employer Client, and Contractor Client).

NOTES ON USE AND COMPLETION

Most projects will be notifiable to the Health and Safety Executive, but the full Regulations will
not be applicable in all cases. However, in nearly every circumstance where an architect is
appointed for work stages involving design, CDM Regulation 13 ('Requirements on designer')
will apply, and this Supplement should be incorporated.

Five additional Definitions are given: CDM Regulations, Health and Safety Plan, Health and
Safety File, Planning Supervisor, Principal Contractor.

There are six additional provisions relating either to the Architect's or to the Client's obligations.
For convenience they are numbered HS.1 to HS.6.

Schedule Two   There are four additional services.

Schedule Three   Where appropriate, an element of the fee relating to compliance with Health and Safety
                            requirements should be identified.

Incorporation   To incorporate the Supplement into the SFA/92 (all versions) it is necessary to make an addition to
                            the Memorandum of Agreement at the second and third points of agreement. These should be
                            amended to read:

                            2   This Appointment is made and accepted on the Conditions of Appointment, Supplementary
                                Provisions and Schedules attached hereto.

                            3   The Architect shall provide the Services specified in Schedule Two and the Supplementary
                                Provisions relating to the Health and Safety CDM Regulations.

Completion   Make sure that the Supplement is dated and initialled by both parties.

                            On the inside front cover of the SFA enter 'CDM Supplement' under **Other documents**.

© 1995 RIBA   4.95 C B A   *Standard Form of Agreement for the Appointment of an Architect (SFA/92)*